Flattery
be damned!

This unique collection of free-wheeling barbs and comebacks teaches you the fine art of insult.

Whether you want to demolish a pest, rib someone, or just raise hell, here's a whole arsenal of wisecracks, lethal lines, and caustic repartee.

Just pick your target, look it up alphabetically, and fire away.

This is the rare book that's both hilarious reading and an indispensable reference tool!

Books by Louis A. Safian

Insults and Puns for Love and Marriage
2,000 Insults for All Occasions
2,000 More Insults

Published by POCKET BOOKS

Most Pocket Books are available at special quantity discounts for bulk purchases for sales promotions, premiums or fund raising. Special books or book excerpts can also be created to fit specific needs.

For details write the office of the Vice President of Special Markets, Pocket Books, 1230 Avenue of the Americas, New York, New York 10020.

2,000

INSULTS
FOR
ALL
OCCASIONS

Compiled by
LOUIS A. SAFIAN

POCKET BOOKS

New York   London   Toronto   Sydney   Tokyo

POCKET BOOKS, a division of Simon & Schuster Inc.
1230 Avenue of the Americas, New York, NY 10020

ISBN: 0-671-70504-0

First Pocket Books printing January 1967

35   34   33   32   31   30

POCKET and colophon are registered trademarks of
Simon & Schuster Inc.

Printed in the U.S.A.

TO MY WIFE REA

*who laughs at all my jokes, not because
they're always clever, but because she is.*

Contents

Introduction

Repartee has been defined as saying what you think after becoming a departee; saying as quick as a flash what you didn't say until next morning. Everyone, at one time or another, has had occasion to echo the familiar lamentation:

> Backward, turn backward, O Time, in your flight,
> I've just thought of a wisecrack I needed last night!

How often have you felt the need at a given moment for a whimsical wisecrack or a waggish quip to put a spark in your conversation? Why be caught with your gags down? You can't win in a battle of wits unless you are properly armed with a repertoire of rapid-fire repartee, a capsule caricature, a salty sally, or a snappy comeback.

The unabashed purpose of this compilation is to enable you, at the drop of a gag, to place your comic, laconic stamps on the idiosyncrasies of diverse specimens of the human race. I have endeavored to include the wit of absurdity, analogy, burlesque, cynicism, drollery, epigram, facetiousness, ridicule, thought-play, word-play and urbanity.

The breezy one-liner, to which I have adhered in this volume, gets your point across in headline form in this age of high speed, sums up a situation in a nutshell, and adds attention-winning punch to your comments. The secret of the success of the epigram is found in its definition—a grain of truth in the twinkling of an eye.

The so-called insult gag is, in essence, an epigrammatic

wisecrack concerning people's nature, conduct, or appearance. TV and nightclub comedians, who are masters of the insult gag, indulge to their hearts' content in acidulous wit and verbal brickbats, bombshells, and blackjacks with the assurance that no one in their audiences identifies himself as their target. Jonathan Swift expressed this idea skillfully in his definition of satire—"a sort of glass, wherein beholders do generally discover everybody's face but their own."

Aside from its reputation for sportive witticism, the insult gag helps at times to blow off steam and get a pet peeve off one's chest. There is an old saying, "It takes all kinds of people to make a world." In our human relations, many of our irritations and annoyances spring from other people's behavior, dress, or appearance. It often becomes necessary to call a spade a spade without stubbing our toes on one.

Edged with the sharp barbs of truth, this thesaurus of sizzling flipquickies, mad-libs, bright slayings, and tongue-whippers offers you a well-stocked arsenal for the fullest expression of your critical faculties. Alphabetically arranged according to the target of your pointed dart, it is a ready reference for assassinating asses, burying boors, demolishing stuffed shirts, knocking the knockers, putting the kibosh on the kibitzers, prodding the pompous, shrinking egotists' heads, and squelching the pest.

So, for your innocent (and not so innocent) pleasure, I offer this supermarket of sweet (and not so sweet) one-liners with which you can add lustre to your reputation as a wit, a clever epigrammist, and an astute caricaturist. The pins are here in abundance to prick a lot of balloons and baboons. With all this ammunition, you can now crack the quips and let them fall where they may.

May your tongue be your sword and may it never grow rusty.

With my best gratings, I am

Very tartly yours,
LOUIS A. SAFIAN

2,000 INSULTS
FOR ALL OCCASIONS

Big Heads

He has gone the way of all flash.

His head is getting too big for his toupee.

His egotism is a plain case of mistaken nonentity.

Every time he opens his mouth, he puts his feats in.

He doesn't want anyone to make a fuss over him—just to treat him as they would any other great man.

He's a real big gun—of small caliber and immense bore.

He'd need a hole in the ground to shrink to his normal proportions.

Someone should press the "down" button on his elevator shoes.

If he had his life to live over again, he would still fall in love with himself.

He thinks it's a halo, but it's only a swelled head.

If his halo falls one more inch, it will be a noose.

He's so bigheaded, he can't get an aspirin to fit him.

He's so conceited, he has his X-rays retouched.

Every time he looks in the mirror, he takes a bow.

He's carrying on a great love affair—unassisted.

His wife worships him—and so does he.

His egotism is nature's compensation for his mediocrity.

Be careful when you're speaking about him—you're speaking of the man he loves.

He's always letting off esteem.

He thinks he's such a shining light, he hands you sunglasses when you look at him.

His conceit is the tribute of a fool.

He's all wrapped up in himself, but he makes a pretty small package.

He's a fellow of real high-hattitude.

He didn't just grow with responsibility—he bloated.

You could make a fortune renting his head out as a balloon.

Success turned his head. Too bad it didn't wring his neck a little.

He thinks he's a big shot just because he explodes.

It's a wonder how such a big head holds such a little mind.

His ego is the only thing about him that kept on growing without nourishment.

He has a 5 ft. 6 in. height and a 6 ft. 5 in. ego.

He's as pompous as an undertaker at a $10,000 funeral.

He's such a big-shot executive, a spiritualist will never be able to contact him. His secretary will have to be contacted first.

You can't help admiring him. If you don't, you're fired.

You can't get anywhere with him by shaking his hand when he puts it out—you have to kiss it.

He doesn't like yes-men around. When he says "No," he wants them to say "No."

He always tells his staff, "Of course, it's only a suggestion, but let's not forget who's making it."

He likes you to come right out and say what you think, when you agree with him.

He's easily entertained. All his staff has to do is just listen to him.

He's always blowing his No's.

He doesn't mind criticism as long as it's out-and-out approval.

He has a colored self-portrait of himself.

He's suffering from infantuation.

Tell him he's brilliant and he says, modestly, "I'll bet you tell that to everyone who's brilliant."

He's so ostentatious, if he ever became an alcoholic, he'd never be admitted to Alcoholics Anonymous.

He's suffering from I-dolatry.

He's an I-soar.

His I's are too close together.

He's an I-specialist.

He's suffering from I-strain.

He's a fellow with big I's who doesn't think of U.

When he meets another egotist, it's an I for an I.

He's a celebrity—spelled "swellebrity."

He's a self-made man who:
- looks more like a warning than an example.
- would have done better if he had let out the contract.
- has no rivals—in love of himself.
- would have been better off if he hadn't been made at all.
- should have consulted an expert.
- adores his maker.
- is the worst example of unskilled labor you've ever seen.
- makes you wonder why he wanted to make himself like that.
- insists on giving everybody the recipe.
- should never have quit the job before it was finished.
- has relieved the Lord of a big responsibility.
- would have been better off if he hadn't fooled around with those do-it-yourself fads.
- believes in himself. Some people are too easily convinced.
- apparently knocked off work too soon.
- never should have hired such cheap labor.
- makes you wonder whether he's boasting or apologizing.

He claims to be the architect of his own success. It's lucky the building inspectors didn't come around during the construction.

From the time he began to be a self-made man, it was the beginning of a lifelong romance.

He's a self-made man whose wife was the power behind the drone.

He wouldn't have done such a good job as a self-made man if his wife hadn't made a few alterations.

His claim that he's self-made sure relieves the conscience of the rest of the world.

You'd make a fortune if you could buy him for what you think of him and sell him for what he thinks of himself.

On his last birthday he sent his parents a telegram of congratulations.

A glazed look comes into his eyes when the conversation drifts away from himself.

He thinks he can push himself forward by patting himself on the back.

His head is so big they have to pin his ears back to get him through Grand Central Station.

His swelled head is just nature's frenzied effort to fill a vacuum.

He's a small country, bounded on the north, south, east, and west by himself.

He's so egotistical, when he hears thunder, he takes a bow.

His conceit is a gift of Providence to a little man.

Take the air out of that little wheel and all you have left is a flat tire.

He's blown his horn so loud, he hasn't any wind left for climbing.

He's high-hatting everyone on the way up. He's liable to meet them on the way down.

One of these days he'll learn that it's only a matter of eighteen inches between a pat on the back and a kick in the pants.

If he ever gets to Heaven he'll find the front seats occupied by fellows who weren't such big shots down here.

As a swelled-up comer, he's a sure goner.

Birthdaze

She's the demure type—demure she gets older, demure she conceals it.

She looks like a million dollars—after taxes.

There'll be no candles on her birthday cake. She's in no mood to make light of her age.

She never forgets her age, once she's decided what it's to be.

She's discovered the secret of perpetual youth—she lies about her age.

If she put the right number of candles on her birthday cake, it would be a fire hazard.

Hoity-toity? She may be hoity, but she'll never see toity again.

Her husband is pleading with her to have birthdays again. He doesn't want to grow old alone.

The best years of her life were the ten years between twenty-nine and thirty.

She's been pressing thirty so long, it's pleated.

Her age ranges from thirty to secrecy.

She could add years to her life by simply telling the truth.

She claims her age is her own business. Poor thing, she's practically out of business.

She reckons her age by light years—she's sure light a few years.

When the census taker asked her how old she was, she couldn't remember whether she was forty-two or forty-three, so she said thirty-five.

She hasn't lost the years she's subtracted from her age; she's just added them to the ages of her sisters-in-law.

Birthdays are occasions that her child deserves, her husband observes, and she preserves.

Birthdays are anniversaries on which her husband takes a day off, and she takes a year off.

She's very loyal. Years ago she reached an age she liked, and she has stuck to it.

When it comes to telling her age, she's shy—about ten years shy.

At twenty-one, she was chosen Miss America. In those days, there were very few Americans.

She won't put the right number of candles on her birthday cake. It wouldn't be a birthday party—it would be a torchlight procession.

She's not what she was fifteen years ago—she's nine years older.

In her opinion, the seven ages of a woman are: baby, infant, junior miss, young woman, young woman, young woman, young woman.

She's aged more than her husband, but less often.

As long as she's capable of juggling figures, she'll never be old.

She uses the count-down method of calculating age.

She's a nice age—thirty-five, especially since she happens to be forty-three.

She has a twin brother who is practically identical, except for one minor detail—he's forty-nine and she's thirty-nine.

Her husband is a diplomat. He remembers her birthday and forgets her age.

When she hesitated to state her age on the witness stand, the judge said, "Hurry, madam, every minute makes it worse."

She's celebrating the tenth anniversary of her thirty-ninth birthday.

She looks like a million—every year of it.

She doesn't object to men who kiss and tell. In fact, at her age she needs all the publicity she can get.

The only time she ever gave her right age was on a safari when she was captured by a fussy cannibal who never ate anyone past forty.

She's in her early flirties.

She knows how to hang on to her youth—she never introduces him to other women.

She finally admitted she was forty, but she didn't say when.

Forty has been the most difficult age for her to pass—it's taken her eight years.

She's living it up, saying, "You're only young once." It's time she thought up some other excuse.

She was eighteen and her husband thirty when they met. Now he's sixty, so she figures since he's twice as old as he was then, she must be thirty-six.

She's afraid to grow old, but at forty she really need have no fear of aging. She'll outgrow it fifteen years from now—when she's forty-eight.

Her hardest decision is when to start middle age.

She wouldn't be trying so hard to conceal her age if her husband would act his.

Her once dangerous curves have become extended detours.

She has stopped exercising—pushing fifty is enough exercise for her.

She's at the age where any man who looks back looks good.

Old blondes never fade—like her, they just dye away.

She worried so much about growing old, she grew blond overnight.

She knew the Big Dipper when it was just a drinking cup.

She knew Heinz when he had only seven varieties.

She knew Howard Johnson when he had only two flavors.

She doesn't have an enemy in the world—she's outlived them all.

She's just gotten a prospectus from an old-age home marked "Urgent."

Boozers

He's suffering from bottle fatigue.

His friends don't know what to get him for Christmas, because they don't know how to wrap up a saloon.

His wife never worries about germs when he kisses her—he's boiled most of the time.

He can get loaded on Scotch tape.

He's drinking to forget. The way he's going at it, he should have complete amnesia in a week.

Life for him is a matter of urps and downs.

Who says he's a hard drinker? He does that easier than anything.

He's working his way down from bottoms up.

He drinks like a fish—too bad he doesn't drink what fishes drink.

When he drinks, he loses his inhibitions and gives exhibitions.

He enjoys cocktail parties where drinks mix people.

With him, two pints make one cavort.

He'd rather be tight than President.

His favorite drink is the next one.

He's a man of high fidelity—staggers home to his wife every night.

He's sot in his ways.

They're going to star him in a move called "The Unquench-ables."

If it wasn't for the olives in the Martinis, he'd starve to death.

He's spoiling his health, drinking to everyone else's.

He enters a bar optimistically, and comes out misty optically.

He's divorcing his wife because she has a sobering effect on him—she hides the bottle.

He's drinking doubles—and seeing the same way.

With him, every day is an alcoholiday.

He graduated from college *magna cum loaded*.

He's writing his autobiography, but it's a hundred quarts too long.

His wife is sticking to him through thick and gin.

His idea of a corking good time is uncorking.

Drinking doesn't just drown his troubles—it irrigates them.

He doesn't only drink—he drinks between drinks.

He'd be the nicest guy on two feet if he could only stay there.

As a kid they called him "Half-pint," but he grew up to be a full quart.

He can always beer up under misfortune.

He thinks Beethoven's Fifth is a bottle.

He's been classified 4A—he's been turned down four times by Alcoholics Anonymous.

He's never been able to join Alcoholics Anonymous—he's never sober enough to memorize the pledge.

Two Scotchmen are ruining him—Haig & Haig.

He has the cutest trick. He walks down the street and turns into a saloon.

He always staggers home the shortest distance between two pints.

He always makes a New Year resolution to stop drinking that goes in one year and out the other.

The Red Cross rejected his blood donation—his plasma had an olive in it.

Those hiccoughs of his are merely messages from departed spirits.

He approaches you from several different directions at once.

He puts vitamins in his gin so he can build himself up while tearing himself down.

His idea of a balanced diet is a highball in each hand.

He's so high, if you smell his breath you get a nosebleed.

After work, he always stops at a bar for an hour and a quart.

He can empty a bottle as quick as a flask.

He has Saloon Arthritis—every night he's stiff in another joint.

When snakes get drunk, they see *him*.

He's drinking something called "Old Maid"—it has no chaser.

He's drinking something called "Card Table"—a couple of them, and his legs fold right up under him.

He has a red nose, a white liver, a green brain, a dark-brown breath, and a blue outlook.

Every New Year he resolves not to drink any more, just about the same.

He's so wet, every time you blow on him he ripples.

He consulted a psychiatrist about his drinking and now things are altogether different—he does his drinking on a couch.

He's in a state of melancholism.

First, he drinks when he's pooped to make a new man out of himself, then he drinks to the new man.

He always goes to parties where there's rum for one more.

He has no respect for age unless it's bottled.

His tippling has a wide range: jocose, morose, bellicose, lachrymose, and comatose.

He started to write a drinking song, but never got past the first two bars.

He was last seen in a bottle of bourbon.

He never drinks more than he can stand—the minute he can stand, he starts drinking again.

Give him a couple of glasses and he's sure to make a spectacle of himself.

He's following his doctor's advice to stop all drinks—you don't see any getting past him.

He's just broken his pledge never to take another drink. It was the worst afternoon he ever spent.

Nothing makes him drink the way he does—he's a volunteer.

With that 100-proof breath, he breathed on his wife's leopard coat and changed it right back to rabbit.

He has cheeks like roses, and a nose to match.

He won't take his doctor's advice to stop drinking. He claims there are lots more old drunks than old doctors.

If you want him to take notice of you, pretend you're a bartender.

The only time he goes to the refrigerator is when he needs ice cubes.

He has a finicky stomach—he can't eat an olive unless it's sterilized in gin.

He's fighting a losing battle trying to keep himself and his business in a liquid condition.

The only way he ever opens a conversation is with a corkscrew.

He saw the ocean for the first time and muttered, "Look at those melted ice cubes."

On board ship, he peered through a porthole all afternoon, finally mumbling, "It'sh a lousy TV show."

On his latest cruise, the weather was so bad he had to be lashed to the bar.

He's thinking of quitting drinking—he's beginning to see the handwriting on the floor.

His head must be made of cork—it's always at the mouth of a bottle.

He thinks he can pull himself out of his troubles with a corkscrew.

He might be able to make both ends meet if he weren't so busy making one end drink.

He's a gin rummy specialist. He drinks so much, he looks like a rummy.

It's a beef-stew marriage. His wife is always beefing and he's always stewed.

It's a nip-and-tuck marriage. He always insists on a nip and his wife has to tuck him in.

If a mosquito bit him, it would die of alcohol-poisoning.

When mosquitoes decide to bite him, they bring along a glass of water as a chaser.

He's been thrown out of so many bars, he now wears nothing but gray, so his suits will match the sidewalk.

He's been dispossessed—they're repairing the gutter.

They're calling him "Cucumber"—he's pickled so often.

They're calling him "Syncopation" because of his irregular movements—from bar to bar.

No wonder his stomach looks like a beer keg—it's all he uses it for.

When he drinks, he feels sophisticated—too bad he can't pronounce it.

The only things he fixes around the house are Manhattans and Martinis.

He only puts on weight in certain places—in saloons, for instance.

All through the day he asks people for the time, and he can't figure out why he always gets different answers.

He magnifies his troubles by looking at them through the bottom of a glass.

He's insulted when you offer him a drink, but he swallows the insult.

He's living proof that there's no fool like an oiled fool.

He reminds you of the proverb "Where there's a swill there's a sway."

He's a perfect illustration of the old saying "A fool and his money are soon potted."

A little blurred never tells him when he's had enough.

He never has a hangover—he stays drunk.

Bores

Only his varicose veins save him from being completely colorless.

If you're enjoying yourself in his company, it's all you're enjoying.

He believes that no matter how crowded a gathering may be, there's room for one bore.

He's so dull, he can't even entertain a doubt.

Monopologues are his specialty.

People and things are here today and gone tomorrow, but he's here today and here tomorrow.

He always has a lot of get-up-and-go except when it's time to get up and go.

As a guest, his shortcoming is his long staying.

As guests go, you wish he would.

He's the kind of neighbor who can get to your house in a minute and out of it in hours.

He comes into a room dragging his tale behind him.

He can stay longer in an hour than most people do in a week.

He's a great athlete—he can throw a wet blanket the entire length of a room.

When there's nothing more to be said, he's still saying it.

He not only monologizes a subject, he monotonizes it.

If you see two fellows together and one looks bored, he's the other.

He has a wide circle of nodding acquaintances.

You have to watch his finger closely—it fits into any buttonhole.

He's hither, thither, and yawn.

There's no doubt he's trying—in fact, he's very trying.

His conversations are on a boast-to-boast hookup.

He deprives you of privacy without providing you with company.

He's interesting to a point—the point of departure.

As his host, you wish he would leave and let live.

He lights up a room when he leaves it.

He says a thousand things, but he never says "good-bye."

He not only encroaches on your time, he trespasses on eternity.

No one is his equal in keeping a conversation ho-humming.

He's full of sayings that should go without saying.

He's as stimulating as a mouthful of sawdust and water.

He's as dull as a fat lapdog after dinner.

The older he gets, the further he descends into his anecdotage.

He can wrap up a one-minute idea in a one-hour vocabulary.

He has a diarrhea of words and a constipation of ideas.

He's such a bore, he couldn't get anyone into his fall-out shelter during a nuclear attack.

You don't know what makes him tick, but you wish it was a time bomb.

He never opens his mouth unless he has nothing to say.

He wearies you with the patter of little feats.

He can get more out of his surgical operation than even Adam did.

It's amazing how he manages to enter a room voice first.

He's very cultured—he can bore you on any subject.

As a host, he makes his company feel at home, and that's where they wish they were.

He throws the kind of party that's a fete worse than death.

His parties are so dull and quiet, you can hear a pun drop.

He's a socialite—one of the Bore Hundred.

He gets offended when others talk while he's interrupting.

He leaves little to your imagination, and even less to your patience.

Chatterboxes

Generally speaking, he's generally speaking.

She must have been vaccinated with a phonograph needle.

He's a sound speaker—and, oh, those sounds!

His idea of conversation is a filibuster.

Her word is never done.

Is she breathtaking! Every few hours she stops talking and takes a breath.

He's the type who approaches every subject with an open mouth.

What he needs is a little lockjaw.

He may be down, but he's never out—talked.

He should rent his mouth out as a fly-catcher.

She not only has the last word, but the last 5,000.

Her vocabulary is small, but the turnover is terrific.

His mouth is so big, he can whisper in his own ear.

He's like a shirt button—always popping off.

She's always giving everyone a preamble to her constitution.

Her tongue is so long, she can seal an envelope after she puts it in the mailbox.

He could talk his head off and never miss it.

Her laryngitis is the wages of din.

He reminds you of a clarinet—a wind instrument.

He has to be eschewed if you don't want to be chewed.

She has a nice, open face—open day and night.

She has a chronic speech impediment—palpitation of the tongue.

He thinks it's more blessed to be glib than to perceive.

The only thing that can cheat her out of a last word is an echo.

Try to argue with him, and his words will flail you.

When you get away from him, you feel like a fugitive from a chin gang.

She's an oft-spoken person.

He's a man of a few words—a few million.

Why, it takes him a half-hour just to say "Hello."

He speaks eight languages, but can't hold his tongue in one.

Everyone calls her "Amazon"—she's so big at the mouth.

They call her "Flo" because she talks in a steady stream.

Her mind is always on the tip of her tongue.

With him, you can't be on speaking terms—unless you're on listening terms.

The last time anyone saw a mouth like his, it had a fishhook in it.

She throws her tongue in high gear before her brain is turning over.

Every time she sets her trap for a man, she forgets to shut it.

He's a freight train of wordage—with no terminal facilities.

If exercise eliminates fat, how in the world did she get that double chin?

What he lacks in depth, he makes up in length—of his tongue.

He knows very little, but he knows it mighty fluently.

She's suffering in silence—her phone is out of order.

He has let his mind go blank, but has forgotten to turn off the sound.

It took her surgeon an hour to perform the operation— it'll take her months to describe it.

He thinks the world will beat a path to his door because he's built a better claptrap.

The way she monopolizes the party line, if anyone needs a doctor they have to put an ad in the paper.

He's very broad-minded—he approaches every question with an open mouth.

You couldn't get a word in with her even if you folded it in two.

His body is getting shorter, but his anecdotes are growing longer.

Her favorite expression is "Oh, I'm speechless!" If she'd only stay that way!

His conversation is as long-drawn-out as the music from an accordion.

When all is said and done—he just keeps on talking.

She talks like a revolving door.

If silence is golden, he must have been born on the silver standard.

He's a real drip. You can always hear him, but can rarely turn him off.

It's no trick for him to put his foot in his mouth—he has a big mouth.

He can hardly ever wait to hear what he's going to say.

He listens to a conversation only when he's talking.

He can be read like a book but not shut up so easily.

When they start a filibuster in Congress, they call him in as an advisor.

What he needs is a yappendectomy.

They call her "A.T. & T."—Always Talking and Talking.

He can even talk for hours about the value of silence.

She's a real vocalamity.

She's getting a double chin—just too much work for one.

The only thing he ever exercises is his tongue.

The best way for her to save face is to keep the lower half shut.

He not only holds a conversation, he strangles it.

She claims to be very outspoken—but she's hardly ever.

She simply loves wordy causes.

He'd be better off if his mind worked as fast as his mouth.

She has a good memory, and a tongue hung in the middle of it.

Chiselers

Whoever molded his character overemphasized the chisel.

He carved his career by first-class chiseling.

He talks on principles and acts on interest.

He's long on promises and short on memory.

In any contract with him, he'll deal from the bottom of the pact.

He always lays his cards on the table, but he has another deck up his sleeve.

He's oilier than a kerosene lamp.

He climbed the ladder of success kissing the feet of the one ahead of him and kicking the head of the one following him.

He's one of those fellows who will pat you on the back before your face and hit you in the face behind your back.

He's a contact man—all con and no tact.

When he says "Good morning," they call the weather bureau to make sure.

He never goes back on his word—without consulting his lawyer.

If he had his conscience taken out, it would be a minor operation.

He's a man of promise—broken promise.

He has as much conscience as a fox in a chicken farm.

When he pats you on the back, he's figuring where to stick the knife.

He's a man of convictions—and he has served time for every one.

He claims he was born with a silver spoon in his mouth. It must have had someone else's initials on it.

Everything he touches turns to gold, but the judge is ordering him to put it back.

He talks in stereophonic style—out of both sides of his mouth.

Even the wool he pulls over your eyes is half rayon.

It's easier to hold an eel by the tail than to pin him down.

He's always ready to back his hot tips with your cash.

He changes sides oftener than a windshield wiper.

He goes through life's revolving door on other people's push.

He reminds you of a bee—a hum-bug.

His friends think they're being cultivated—but they're being trimmed.

He's as elusive as a wet fish.

He has the gift of grab.

He prays on his knees on Sunday, and on everybody the rest of the week.

He stands for everything he thinks you'll fall for.

He's going to Saranac for respiratory trouble; his creditors won't let him breathe easy.

If he enters into a verbal contract with someone for $200 a week, he pays off verbally.

He's an expert at handing out baloney disguised as food for thought.

He has a lot of grit. He can take it—no matter who owns it.

He's a human kite. He got where he is with wind and pull.

He's polished—in a slippery sort of way.

He has the human touch; it conceals an itching palm.

He started out in life as an unwanted child—now he's wanted in ten states.

Give him a free hand and he'll stick it right in your pocket.

He was born a mountaineer and hasn't been on the level since.

If you lend him money, you can charge it to profit and louse.

When he pats you on the back, he's trying to get you to cough up something.

He's a big iron and steel man from Pittsburgh. His wife irons and he steals.

The louder he protests his honesty, the more firmly you have to clasp your wallet.

Honesty pays for most people, but it doesn't pay enough to suit *him*.

When he lays his cards on the table, it's a good idea to count them.

He got his principal entirely without principle.

Watch out when he shakes your hand; he's trying to pump money out of your pocket.

When he left his last apartment, his landlady actually wept —he owed six months' rent.

He got that stoop living up to his ideals.

You're safe while he holds you warmly by both your hands —because you can watch both of his.

His ancestors never made an honest dollar and he's following in their fingerprints.

He's such a phoney, he even gets cavities in his false teeth.

If he was a psychologist, he'd be another Fraud.

He has one of those hydromatic handshakes—no clutch.

Some men marry poor women to settle down. He's marrying a rich one to settle up.

He's so tricky, he could skin a flint.

His paycheck should be gift-wrapped.

His remarks are always more candied than candid.

He's a gentleman to his fingerprints.

The only time he calls a spade a spade is when he stubs his toe on one.

A dollar can never fall as low as the means he adopted to get it.

He gives publicly and steals privately.

When he was a boy, his ambition was to be a pirate. It isn't everyone that realizes his ambitions.

He's always ready to help you get what's coming to him.

He's so sugary, you can get diabetes listening to him.

He claims that once, in Europe, he called on three kings. It must have been in a poker game.

His credit is so bad, he can't even borrow trouble.

He can put the screws on you faster than an undertaker.

He believes in the greatest good for the greatest number, and his idea of the greatest number is Number One.

As far as he's concerned, the voice of Conscience has no telling effect.

He's pulling himself up by his bootlicks.

He was recently voted "Man of the Hour"—but you've got to watch him every minute.

He's one of those get-rich-quick schemers who's always on the lookout for people who want to get poor quick.

He's as hypocritical as a funeral director trying to look sad at a $10,000 funeral.

He likes to eat his cake and have yours too.

He's very generous with his friends. He'll always divide with them—as much as they have.

He's as phoney as a dentist's smile.

He's living from handout to mouth.

He lives by the sweat of his frau.

He's leading a dog's life—creditors are dogging his footsteps.

He gets awfully depressed when he sees his friends spending money lavishly and he can't help them.

The less you have to do with him, the less you'll be worse off.

You can always get from him straight-from-the-shoulder double-talk.

If you pieced together all the bum checks he writes in a month, you'd have a good-sized rubber raincoat.

He married a woman for her pa value.

He has a magnetic personality. Everything he has is charged.

You have to have good blood pressure watching how free he is with the money he owes you.

He never forgets a favor—if he did it.

He's as artificial as manufactured ice.

His wife likes to shop on the sunny side of the street, but he prefers to do his business on the shady side.

He's done a good deal for lots of people. He's kept a flock of detectives, bill collectors, and Treasury men working regularly.

As a young fellow, he once ran away with a circus, but the police caught him and made him bring it back.

He has a lot of hidden charms; his money is in vaults, in Swiss banks, and so on.

He is a master of the art of moving in best circles without going straight.

He buys lovely period furniture—and it's only a short period before the installment people take it back.

One time he was connected with the police department—by a pair of handcuffs.

He's always selling himself. The trouble is he misrepresents the goods.

He has a positive genius for worming his way out of your confidence.

He claims his furniture goes back to Louis the 14th. It will, if he doesn't pay Louis before the 14th.

He's so full of angles, he's selling haunting licenses to ghosts.

He's a real phoney—a cross between nothing.

If he ever fell over his own bluff, he'd be fractured.

He seems to be too good to be true—and he isn't.

He claims he lost a wad at the races. Next time he shouldn't bet chewing gum.

He tells women he's loaded with the green stuff—he's a lettuce farmer.

He claims he has enough money to live on for the rest of his life, and he has, too—if he died next week.

He claims his sofa is French Provincial 1809, but it's Sears Roebuck—$395.

He claims his dad is a Southern planter. For once he's telling the truth—his dad is a Mississippi undertaker.

He claims he's a big man—has several hundred people under him. He's a watchman in a cemetery.

He claims he used to be an organist but gave it up. His monkey must have died.

He claims he was once a lifeguard. It must have been in a car wash.

He claims he comes from a family of standing. They're probably floorwalkers, elevator operators, and policemen.

He claims he comes from a family of rock 'n' rollers. They hit you on the head and then they roll you.

He claims the coat he got his wife is dyed mink. From the looks of it, it must have died a horrible death.

His oily tongue goes with his slick mind.

He's as phoney as a harlot's tears.

He's as deceitful as a crow.

His probity is all right—until someone probes.

If you lend him money, you never see him again—and it's worth it.

If you lend him your garden rake, he cames back for mower.

He believes in free speech—especially long distance phone calls on other people's phones.

He says he has followed the Ten Commandments all his life. Too bad he never managed to catch up with them.

He has the kind of checkered career that's bound to end up in a striped suit.

He left the farm because he was sure that the Man with the Hoe doesn't get nearly as far as the Man with the Hokum.

Crabs

He's so disagreeable, his own shadow won't keep him company.

He's so contrary, he does everything versa vice.

You can't tell him anything—he has a soundproof head.

He follows the straight and narrow-minded path.

He's so narrow-minded, he can look through a keyhole with both eyes.

He's so narrow-minded, he has to stack his ideas vertically.

She's the kind of hostess whom you thank for her hostility.

Arguing with her is like trying to read a newspaper in a high wind.

He's a blower-upper without any countdown.

He has a concrete mind—permanently set and all mixed up.

She's so contrary, if she drowned they'd have to look upstream for her.

He looks through rose-colored glasses with a jaundiced eye.

His tactics are a combination of needles and threats.

34

He likes people who come right out and say what they think, when they agree with him.

He doesn't like Yes-men. He doesn't mind anyone disagreeing with him, even though it costs them their job.

He had three phones installed, so he can hang up on more people.

He's a real lamb; when you ask him for a raise, he says, "Ba-a-a-ah."

Everyone has a good word for him—they all whisper it.

He has an open mind—it should be closed for repairs.

Arguing with him is like trying to blow out an electric-light bulb.

It's as easy to convince him as trying to poultice the hump off a camel's back.

He's always down on everything he's not up on.

He believes in law and order—just so long as he can lay down the law and give the order.

He has a disposition like an untipped waiter.

He claims he never made a mistake in his life, but he has a wife who did.

There's nothing wrong with him that trying to reason with him won't aggravate.

His comebacks are as snappy as his checks.

He thinks the world is against him—and it is.

He's as cross as capital X . . . as irascible as a sick monkey . . . as surly as a butcher's dog . . . as cross as a child denied a sugarplum.

He can make more cutting remarks than a tax examiner.

He's a very determined person. When he puts his foot down, someone is invariably under it.

One of these days he'll really lose his head, and the chances are he'll never miss it.

To a guy with a sour puss like his, you don't say "Good morning"; you say "Unhappy days."

He's as uncompromising as a policeman's club.

He should have been an auctioneer—he looks forbidding.

He's been peevish ever since as a boy he crawled under a tent to see the circus, and found it was a revival meeting.

He's so technical, if you should sneeze at a board meeting and someone said, *"Gesundheit,"* he'd put it to a vote.

She's all right in her own way—but she always wants it.

She has the kind of intuition that enables her to put two and two together and come up with an answer that suits her.

She claims to be positive, but she's just wrong at the top of her voice.

The only time she'll listen to an argument is when it's by her next-door neighbors.

First thing in the morning she brushes her teeth and sharpens her tongue.

She belongs to the meddle classes.

She thinks marriage is a good investment if, as a mother-in-law, she puts her two cents in.

He entertains new thoughts as if they were his in-laws.

He pays you a compliment like he expected a receipt.

He reminds you of a crocodile; when he opens his mouth,

you don't know whether he's trying to smile or getting ready to chew you up.

Whatever is eating him must be suffering from indigestion.

He has a unique talent for invading an issue.

They call him "Sliver" because he's always getting under everyone's skin.

If he's ever forced to eat his own words, he'll have an acute case of indigestion.

He's always as sore as a porcupine with ingrown quills.

He's as tranquil as a Texas cyclone.

He's temperamental—90 per cent temper and 10 per cent mental.

He's a very sneer-sighted person.

When he wants your opinion, he gives it to you.

He's always sticking his No's in other people's business.

He's running a large-scale operation with a small-scale mind.

When he weighs facts, he's sure to have his thumbs on the scale.

There's an explanation for his disposition—he must have sized himself up recently and gotten awfully sore about it.

When he became the department head, they replaced the office sign reading "Smile" with a new one reading "Smile Anyway."

The way he barks at you, you'd think you were his old father or mother.

He doesn't pull his own weight as much as he throws it around.

His idea of stimulating sales is to stick pins into his salesmen instead of into the maps.

His idea of efficiency is placing signs all over the office: "Remember, you can be replaced by a button."

He doesn't hold an opinion—it holds him.

He won't even listen to both sides of a phonograph record.

He's generous to a fault—when it's his own.

The trouble with him is that someone once told him to be himself.

The more his teeth drop out, the more biting he gets.

He'd find faults even in Paradise.

The less he knows, the more stubbornly he knows it.

The narrower his mind, the broader his statements.

He's a genius at arguing about things he doesn't understand.

The only time he listens to reason is to gain time for a rebuttal.

He's not feeling so well. Something he agreed with is eating him.

He's one of those cynics who thinks the world never changes—just short-changes.

You have as much chance of winning an argument with him as with an umpire.

When he was seven, he found there was no Santa Claus and he's been cynical ever since.

He thinks twice before he speaks, so that he can say something nastier than if he spoke right out.

He thinks he's broad-minded, but he's really thick-headed.

He's always giving you a piece of his mind, and he can least afford it.

You often wonder whether the chip is on his shoulder or in his head—or both.

He must have gotten up on the wrong side of the floor this morning.

They call him "the Compositor"—he has such set ways.

The hardest thing he finds to give is in.

He's as stimulating as a hearse . . . as a graveyard on a wet Sunday . . . as a squeezed lemon . . . as a subpoena.

He has an even disposition—always waspish, cross, crusty, and crabbed.

He's leading his staff such a rat race, they're on a strike for more cheese.

Cream Puffs

He wouldn't even open an oyster without first knocking on the shell.

He's regular Rock of Jello.

Once he makes up his mind, he's full of indecision.

He does everything the *herd* way.

He's not a Yes-man. When the boss says No, *he* says No.

With him, necessity is the mother of tension.

He's so nervous, he keeps coffee awake.

He's never been married—he's just a self-made mouse.

His trouble is too much bone in the head and not enough in the back.

He's living in the present—tense.

He's so tense, his office furniture is overwrought iron.

He's as spineless as a chocolate eclair.

After they made him, they broke the jelly mold.

He's as nervous as a cat up a tree.

He won't wear contact lenses. What would he put on in case a fight started?

He has as much guts as a skeleton.

They call him "Jigsaw." Every time he's faced with a problem, he goes to pieces.

He's so indecisive, when his psychiatrist asked him if he had trouble making up his mind, he answered, "Yes and no."

He works so hard because he's too nervous to steal.

These smoking reports are making him so nervous, he's smoking twice as much.

He reminds you of a weathercock that turns with every wind.

He's in constant fear his last breath will be a hiccough, and he won't be able to say "Excuse me."

He's always on the fence to avoid giving offense.

What he needs more than his intercom system is an inner calm system.

Brave? He'll go into the morgue and offer to lick any man in the house.

Once while hunting in Africa he bagged a lion—he bagged and bagged him to please go away.

He's just found a job that takes a lot of guts—he strings tennis racquets.

He never takes tranquilizers—if he's not tense, he's nervous.

He always stoops to concur.

His ulcers are not from what he eats, but what's eating him.

He's the real decisive type—he'll always give you a definite maybe.

Whenever he feels like disagreeing with the boss, he first looks at both sides—his side and the outside.

His psychiatrist just told him, "You haven't got an inferiority complex—you are inferior."

He has a lot of courage—to bear the misfortunes of others.

He's so timid, he tells an elevator operator, "The 22nd floor, please, if it won't take you out of your way."

He's as nervous as a diner watching the chef handling a racing form.

He's so nervous, he twangs in a high wind.

They call him "Serutan" because he's so backward.

He has a unique talent for making difficulties out of opportunities.

His final decision seldom tallies with the one immediately following it.

He's so indecisive, he has a seven-year-old son he hasn't named yet.

He's as jumpy as a kangaroo, as fidgety as an old maid, and as pliable as wax.

He bows and scrapes like a windshield wiper.

He gives his conscience a lot of credit that belongs to his cold feet.

He's a man of conviction—after he knows what his wife thinks.

Dressed and Undressed

Her gowns are cut to see level.

Give her an inch and she'll soon wear it for a dress.

She wears a $200 gown, but her heart isn't in it.

In choosing her evening gowns, she goes practically all out.

She wears too much of not enough.

She has reached success by attireless effort.

The way she wears clothes, she can't even hide her embarrassment.

Her clothes are based on the assumption that men find a woman least wearing when she wears least.

She wears peek-a-bosom gowns.

She dresses to be seen in the best places.

She wears the kind of dresses that start late and end early.

Her evening gowns are real confusing. You can't decide whether she's on the inside trying to get out, or on the outside trying to get in.

She shows more of a lot of woman than a lot of style.

She wears Texas dresses—with those wide, open spaces.

The way her neckline keeps going down and her hemline keeps going up, the fellows are all hanging around; they want to be there when both ends meet.

She looks as if she was poured into her dress and forgot to say when.

She's a moron with less on.

She's *Vogue* on the outside and vague on the inside.

She wears atom-bomb dresses—a 50 percent fall-out.

The way she dresses, every day is the dawn of a nude day for her.

She's fast gaining a reputation for being the less-dressed woman in town.

She wears the kind of gown that is more gone than gown.

She wears so little, farmers want to hire her to shock their grain.

Her clothes are designed not so much to make her look good as to make men look good.

She's dressed like she's fleeing from a burning building.

She wears unmentionables—nothing to speak of.

With those low-cut dresses, it doesn't take much talking on her part to pour her heart out.

She wears more clothes when she goes to bed than when she goes out evenings.

Her clothes fit her—like a convulsion.

Her neckline is so low, you can't tell whether her dress is slipping or she's coming up.

Her clothes are like barbed wire—they protect the property without obstructing the view.

The only time she has something on is when she dresses a wound, or has a coat on her tongue.

She has no more on her body than on her mind.

She made it to the top because her clothes didn't.

Just one false move she'll make in that dress—and the boys will appreciate it.

That strapless gown can never, never survive the next samba.

Her dresses are like racing cars—they hold fast going around the curves.

It would do her some good, once in awhile to stop, look, and loosen.

She dresses like a bad photograph—overdeveloped and overexposed.

She's either suffering from clothestrophobia, or she likes life in the raw.

She's penny-wise and gowned foolish.

She's looking for the impossible—a fashion designer who can make a dress both fitting and proper.

She looks as if her clothes were thrown on her with a pitchfork.

She's a regular clotheshorse. When she puts on her clothes, she looks like a horse.

Her wardrobe ensemble is in a clash by itself.

She's not just dressed—she's upholstered.

Nothing is harder on her clothes than another woman's.

She has absolutely nothing to wear, and three closets to keep it in.

Her entire conversation consists of who, what, when, and wear.

She's always at the beach trying to outstrip the other girls.

She goes to the seashore, where she puts on a bikini and takes off her brains.

She goes to the beach with a baiting suit.

She wears two bandanas and an unworried look.

She wears the kind of bikini that's based on theory that nothing succeeds like nothing.

Her bathing suit is designed to enable her to clink or swim.

A moth would have to be on a strict diet to eat her bathing suit.

She's a living example of a stern reality—a plump dame in shorts.

She wears clinging dresses. The ones she's wearing have been clinging to her for years.

That's a nice dress she's wearing. Her friends wonder if the style will ever come back.

She never follows a new fashion unless it's impractical, uncomfortable, and unbecoming.

She has a passion for clothes, none of which return her affection.

If that's mink she's wearing, some rabbit must be living under an assumed name.

She dresses in season—like an Easter egg or a Christmas tree.

Her hat looks as if it had made a forced landing on her head.

With those silly hats she wears, it's obvious she's the one who wears the plants in the family.

She says that whenever she's down in the dumps she gets a new hat. Obviously that's where she gets them.

She looks as bedraggled as a pigeon who got caught in a badminton game.

She's as up to date as a 1940 calendar.

She dresses to please, and it doesn't take much to please her.

Her slacks are so tight, she has to carry her handkerchief in her mouth.

She's interested in clothes—too bad she's not interesting in them.

As the first duck said to the second duck, "Stop walking like that dame wearing slacks."

She's in her salad days—but she's not very particular about her dressing.

She's dressed like an unmade bed.

She must be wearing those clothes to pay off an election bet.

Her clothes look as though she'd dressed in front of an airplane propeller.

She has a suit for every day in the month—the one she has on.

There's something that won't go with that loud dress of hers —her husband.

She's as seedy as a raspberry.

Her friends hadn't seen her for four years. If it wasn't for her dress they never would have recognized her.

Dumbbells

The closest he'll ever come to a brainstorm is a light drizzle.

Brains aren't everything. In fact, in her case they're nothing.

They've named a town after him—Marblehead, Massachusetts.

He's going to the hospital for a minor operation—they're putting a brain in.

The only thing that can stay in his head more than an hour is a cold.

He doesn't dare be lost in thought. He's a total stranger there.

When she says "Hello," she tells you all she knows.

If he said what he thought, he'd be speechless.

She has no more on her mind than anywhere else.

He spends half his time trying to be witty. You might say he's a half-wit.

They call her "Sanka" because she has no active ingredient in the bean.

It takes her an hour to cook Minute rice.

He'd have to climb Mt. Everest to reach a deep thought.

Every time he gets into a taxi, the driver keeps the "Vacant" sign up.

He lost his mind when a butterfly kicked him in the head.

He's an M.D.—Mentally Deficient.

He's just gotten an idea. He should be real kind to it—it's a long way from home.

A demitasse would fit his head like a sombrero.

Too bad they don't sell toupees with brains in them.

He goes to a chiropodist for psychoanalysis—his brains are in his feet.

His brain is like a politician's speech—mostly empty.

The only reason he manages to keep his head above water is that wood floats.

He can detect a rattle in his car quicker than one in his head.

The only way he'll lose a lot of fat is to cut his head off.

She was hurt while taking a milk bath. The cow slipped and fell on her head.

He's such a blockhead, he gets a sliver in his fingers every time he scratches his head.

He has a brain—but it hasn't reached his head.

He was born stupid, and lately he's had a relapse.

He's brighter than he looks—but then, he'd just have to be.

He couldn't count up to twenty without taking his shoes off.

He's full of brotherly love. He always stops anyone who's beating a donkey.

He has a lot of backbone. The trouble is, the bone is all on the top.

Scientists are studying how long a man can live without brains. They're checking his age.

He claims he just got a bright idea—beginner's luck!

Dieting won't help him—no diet will reduce a fathead.

He may talk like a fool and act like a fool. But don't get the wrong idea about him—he *is* a fool.

He's the living proof of reincarnation. No one could be as dumb as he in one lifetime.

Everything that's said to her goes into one ear and out the other—there's nothing to block traffic.

He'd have to step out of his mind to get an idea.

Everything about her is open—an open mind with a vacant stare.

The last time he stuck his head out of his basement door, they started a hockey game.

He was so excited when he was promoted from the sixth to the seventh grade, he could hardly shave without cutting himself.

She has a soft heart, and a head to match.

At school he had underwater marks—below C level.

He has a photographic mind, but nothing develops.

What he lacks in intelligence he makes up in stupidity.

He has a mind like a defective parachute—it doesn't open when it should.

Everyone keeps telling him to put his best foot forward. The trouble is, he doesn't know which one it is.

He always stops to think. The trouble is, he forgets to start again.

If they ever put a price on his head, he should take it.

She's more concerned with what's on her head than what's in it.

He's a fugitive from a brain gang.

He's just as smart as he can be—unfortunately.

He can never seem to make up what little mind he has left.

He's a man of rare intelligence—it's rare when he shows any.

He's like a blotter—takes it all in but gets it backwards.

He would do well to follow the example of his head and come to the point.

He's a gross ignoramus—144 times worse than an ordinary ignoramus.

He goes through life believing everything; it saves him from thinking.

He says he's going to give up working and live by his wits. Well, half a living is better than none.

Noises in his head never keep him awake. You can't transmit sound through a vacuum.

Every time there's fire in his eyes it's quenched by the water on his brain.

His mind wanders, and he just goes along.

He's a simple man of the people—in fact, the simplest.

He has been educated beyond his intelligence.

Poor guy, in a battle of wits he's completely unarmed.

It's not that he hasn't presence of mind; his trouble is absence of thought.

He's got brains, but they're in dead storage.

It looks like he'll never be too old to learn new ways of being stupid.

On a recent aptitude test, he not only had every answer wrong—he even misspelled his name.

The only fast way he'll ever broaden his mind is to put it under a train.

He's nobody's fool. Poor guy, he couldn't get anyone to adopt him.

He speaks straight from the shoulder. Too bad his remarks don't start higher up.

The breakfast room of a honeymoon hotel isn't as vacant as his head.

She has a heart of gold and a brain of pure meringue.

He isn't a chip off the old block—he's the old block itself.

The programs she watches on TV are a vidiot's delight.

She's even stuck for an answer when someone says "Hello."

Offer him a penny for his thoughts and you're more than liberal.

It's a mystery how his head grew without any nourishment.

He's like an old stove—big belly and no head.

They're trying to find a job for him one step below automation.

He has most situations right in the hollow of his head.

She has a 40 bust and an I.Q. to match.

If there's an idea in his head, it's in solitary confinement.

When he was in the eighth grade he wasn't at all like any of the other kids—maybe that was because he was eighteen.

He was in one class so long, the other pupils used to bring him apples thinking he was the teacher.

At college he was a halfback and away back in his studies. His college education was only pigskin deep.

There's a fable about an ass disguising himself with a lion's skin, but his college did it for him with a sheepskin.

His dad backed his college education with thousands of dollars, and all he got was a quarterback.

He went to college to develop his mind—too bad he's never used it.

He's so gullible, he buys a hair restorer from a bald barber.

He's the exception to the rule that man is the only animal that can't be skinned more than once.

For him, especially, someone should invent a Sucker Fountain Pen—one that runs dry when it comes to signing on the dotted line.

He's as blank as an empty bottle, as dizzy as a goose, and as stupid as a coot.

It takes real talent to be as dumb as he is.

He says he's changed his mind. Too bad his new mind doesn't work any better than the old one.

She's got a terrific stairway, but not much upstairs.

If you want to point out a concrete example, ask him to remove his hat.

He's not exactly dumb, but he was fourteen years old before he could wave good-bye.

If he has a cold or something in his head, it's a cold.

He has an ironclad defense against the impact of new ideas —stupidity.

He kept learning more and more about less and less, until now he knows everything about nothing.

He won't submit to an operation for the removal of excess fat. He refuses to have himself beheaded.

He reminds you in a way of the Beatles—he doesn't have a forehead.

He's at his wit's end, and it hasn't taken him long to get there.

There's one thing you can say for him. He's come a long way—for a nincompoop.

The job interviewer said to him, "Yes, we do have an opening for you—and don't slam the door on your way out."

He was born dumb, and it's amazing how he's expanded his birthright.

He wears blue ties to match his blue eyes, and soft hats to match his head.

The way he plays the market, he's neither a bull nor a bear—just a jackass.

He has a successful substitute for lack of brains—silence.

He comes from a long line of real estate people—they're a vacant lot.

His biggest stumbling block is the one under his hat.

Light travels at the rate of 186,000 miles per second, and it hasn't yet reached his mind.

Whoever said it's impossible to underrate human intelligence must have had him in mind.

They use him as a mold for making dumbbells.

He kept his mouth shut and everyone thought him a nincompoop; then he opened it and removed all doubt.

If he had a little more sense he'd be a half-wit.

He has just taken an aptitude test. Good thing he owns the company.

Anyone can be lost in a fog, but he creates his own.

Human intelligence is said by scientists to be half a million years old. In his case, it still isn't large enough for its age.

She called the Fidelity Insurance Company to have her husband's fidelity insured.

He returned a Louis XIV bed because it was too small, and asked for a Louis XV.

He broke a mirror to be sure he'd live another seven years.

He took out blanket insurance because he smokes in bed.

He won't buy a fall-out shelter now. He says he'll wait and buy a used one later.

She added a TV aerial to her washing machine to get cleaner reception.

He put a cake of ice in front of his safe so burglars would get cold feet.

She was asked what she thought of Red China and she said, "It's all right as long as it doesn't clash with the tablecloth."

She thought she was pregnant, so she swallowed some blank film so nothing would develop.

He'd stick his head in an oven to get a baked bean.

She's been cooking the chicken two days because the cookbook said to cook one half-hour to the pound and she weighs 110 pounds.

She was asked if she liked Kipling and she answered, "I don't know—I've never kippled."

He takes off his coat when he weighs himself—and holds it on his arm to get his correct weight.

The preacher told him to spread some sunshine at every opportunity, so he's going around with a sun lamp.

All he knows about nitrates is that they're cheaper than day rates.

He's been working on an invention—crossing a rabbit with a piece of lead to get a repeating pencil.

He's running around a cracker box because its wrapping reads: "Tear around the top."

They tell her she has a silly puss and she insists she doesn't have a crazy cat.

He's looking around for a round mailbox so he can post a circular letter.

He dips his finger in the glass first to make sure he's got a soft drink.

He boasts that his kid can already say "Dada"—and he's only eight years old.

People told him they'd like to see some change in him, so he swallowed five pennies.

She called the Community Chest for an appointment to have her chest examined.

He bought a truck farm because he heard there's a lot of money in selling trucks.

He thought his wife had stopped smoking cigarettes because he found cigar butts around the house.

She lists her hats as deductible expenses on her tax returns because they "are overhead."

He listed their unborn baby on his tax report because it was part of last year's work.

He heard that the dollar's value is decreasing and the price of bread is going up, so he saves bread.

He followed a wagon-sprinkler down the street for a mile to tell the driver his wagon was leaking.

She got rid of her refrigerator because it was too much trouble to cut ice into those little squares to fit into the trays.

Watching the toe dancers at a ballet, he wanted to know why they didn't get taller girls.

A fellow told her she'd learn to love him in time, so she's keeping his picture in her watch.

He went to the movies to see "The Desert" and asked for two tickets in the shade.

He won't buy insurance, because his dad had a $50,000 insurance policy and it didn't do him any good—he died anyway.

She was going abroad, and when she went to her doctor for shots, she slapped him when he asked to see her itinerary.

He won't buy an electric toothbrush because he doesn't know whether his teeth are A.C. or D.C.

He found a derby in his apartment and sued for divorce on the ground that he couldn't live with a woman who wears a derby.

He puts starch in his cocktails so that he can have a good stiff drink.

When he heard of short-wave reception, he bought a midget radio.

He went to a nudist camp for a game of strip poker.

He went to a nudist camp to sell subscriptions to a fashion magazine.

He wanted to raise a litter of puppies, so he planted a piece of dogwood.

He took the car out in a rainstorm because it was a driving rain.

She thinks the Ford Foundation is a new kind of girdle.

He tried to buy the hat-check concession in an Orthodox synagogue.

She was insulted because a fellow asked her if she was familiar with *Gray's Anatomy*.

He went to the zoo to see what a Christmas seal looks like.

He didn't stay for the second act of the play because it said on the program: "Act 2, two weeks later."

He left the theater at the end of the second act because the program read: "Act 3: same as Act 2."

He looked for a get-well card in the German language because his friend had German measles.

He doesn't see the need to buy toothpaste because his teeth aren't loose.

She brought her cosmetics for a make-up exam.

He applied for insurance because if his hair fell out, the policy would cover his head.

He sleeps at the edge of the bed so that he can drop right off.

He won't buy Webster's Dictionary until they make it into a movie.

He rejected a nose insurance policy because it wasn't printed on Kleenex.

If someone lifts his coffee cup and says *"Skoal,"* he says, "No, it's hot."

He stayed on the phone an hour trying to get "Established 1894."

He had a pair of bloomers tattooed on his chest because he always wanted a chest with drawers.

She told her children they could watch the solar eclipse but not to get too close.

He's afraid to eat an apple because he heard his uncle died of "appleplexy."

Besides being so dumb, he's also a tightwad and a woman-chaser, so he went to Reno because he heard it's a place where women are made free.

She's so dumbly superstitious she turned down a marriage proposal because she was reading *The Birth of a Nation* at the time.

He stands in front of the mirror with his eyes closed to see what he looks like when he's asleep.

He keeps looking down all the time because his doctor told him to watch his stomach.

His bride had to postpone the honeymoon so she could explain to him what it was.

He stuffs his mattress with billiard balls so he can roll out of bed.

He takes a pint to bed with him so he can sleep tight.

Passing through customs, he was asked if he any pornographic literature, and he said, "I haven't even got a pornograph."

Entertainers

His performance has to be seen and heard to be depreciated.

She acts with as much feeling as a fresh-frozen stalk of asparagus.

He comes from a family with a turn for music—they were organ-grinders.

He should be given mustard gas—it goes good with ham.

He's such a ham, no wonder he's critics' meat.

He's living from ham to mouth.

The entire audience was hissing him, except one man. He was applauding the hissing.

She's a promising singer—she should promise to stop singing.

She has a nice voice. In time it may reach her throat.

Her voice is like a drowned seaman—it dies at C.

Her rendition was a howling success.

Instead of singing "The Road to Mandalay," he should have taken it.

He gave a very moving performance—everyone moved to the nearest exit.

Her singing was mutiny on the high C's.

She claims she insured her voice for $100,000. It would be interesting to know what she did with the money.

The audience called for him after his performance, and if it hadn't been for the riot squad they would have gotten him.

He gave the same performance five nights running—he wouldn't dare giving it standing still.

His audience was with him all the way—no matter how fast he ran, he couldn't shake them.

She's a straight actress—36-36-36.

His audience was real polite—they covered their mouths when they yawned.

He's a mastoid of ceremonies—a pain in the neck.

What a comedian! When he performs, the nightclub waives the amusement tax.

What an ad libber! He couldn't even have an argument with anyone without a TelePrompTer.

He was a pioneer on radio. He was the first to be turned off.

He's an M.C. all right—a Mental Case.

She has a singular voice. Good thing it isn't plural.

The way she hits that high C, it sounds as though the high C hits back.

With a voice like hers, if she sang in a cage full of lions, the ASPCA would get after her.

He put his heart and soul into the rendition. Too bad he couldn't put a little music into it too.

She has a nice voice. She ought to cultivate it—and then plant potatoes in it.

He played Macbeth. Macbeth lost.

Her performance underwhelmed the audience.

The only reason he wasn't hissed is that the audience couldn't yawn and hiss at the same time.

She claims singing warms the blood. Hers makes ours boil.

There's only one explanation for that voice—he gargles with ground glass.

In his last appearance at a theater he drew a line three blocks long, but they took his chalk away.

He developed his singing in the bathtub. Maybe he should take more baths.

As a comedian, he couldn't get a laugh out of a laughing hyena.

You don't dare call for an encore—he might call your bluff.

The only explanation for his being an actor is that he likes to sleep late.

After his performance the audience shouted, "Fine! Fine!" —and darned if he didn't have to pay it.

He has discontinued singing on account of his throat. His audiences have threatened to cut it.

What a ventriloquist! His dummy is quitting him to find a new partner.

As an orchestra conductor, he doesn't know his brass from his oboe.

His audiences are glued to their seats. One of these days he'll run out of mucilage.

If the rumor has any foundation, she was made for the part.

She has no talent for acting but she's too famous to give it up.

She insists she's an artist. Her considerate friends are keeping her secret.

As a nightclub singer, she's worth watching. Too bad she's not worth listening to.

After the final curtain, he held hands with the rest of the cast for fear if they broke loose, one of them would have to take the consequences.

He belongs to a five-piece band—they know only five pieces.

He gives the kind of performance that gives failure a bad name.

His repertoire needs scissors and taste.

Her performance had a happy ending—the curtain finally rang down.

His nightclub act starts at 11:30 sharp and ends at 12:30 dull.

There are said to be only twelve basic jokes. Listening to him, you wonder what happened to the other eleven.

He says he dreams his material—how he must dread going to bed.

He hasn't had a role in three years, but he can't give up acting because it's his living.

With the advent of television, an entire new field of unemployment opened up for him.

Failures

He had a forward spring—and an early fall.

When opportunity knocked at his front foor, he was out in the backyard looking for four-leaf clovers.

He has both feet firmly planted in the air.

He has spent his whole life in the development of one part of his body—the wishbone.

He's a jack-of-all-trades, and out of work in all of them.

He has a B.A., an M.A., and a Ph.D., but no J.O.B.

He has always followed the path of least persistence.

He goes through life pushing doors marked "Pull."

When he was young he was determined to climb the ladder of success. He's not so successful, but, boy! can he climb ladders!

He has risen from obscurity and is headed for oblivion.

Years ago he was an unknown failure—now he's a known failure.

He lacks only three things to get to the top: talent, ambition, and initiative.

He has a fat chance to succeed, and a head to match.

He's like a pin without a head—always getting into things beyond his depth.

He's on the right track, but he's getting run over sitting there.

He has more pipe dreams than an organist.

He's very responsible. No matter what goes wrong, he's always responsible.

The way he manages his money—confidentially, it shrinks.

He's broke more often than a New Year's resolution.

He's as broke as a pickpocket at a nudist camp.

Everyone calls him the "Archeologist" because his career lies in ruins.

He's going to the dogs faster than a flea.

He gives failure a bad name.

Some day he's going to find himself—and will he be disillusioned!

His trouble is in trying to run large-scale operations with a small-scale mind.

He's always undertaking vast projects with half-vast ideas.

He always blew his own horn so much, it didn't leave him any wind for climbing.

He's all sail and no anchor.

He's a human dynamo who got short-circuited along the way.

He never makes the same mistake twice. Every day he finds some new mistakes to make.

The only way he'll ever get up in the world is in an airplane.

His mother told him that when he grew up, he would come out on top, and she was right—he's bald-headed.

He has something to fall back on, and it won't be long before he lands on it.

He started business on a shoestring and took a lacing.

If a pickpocket went through his pockets, all he would get is exercise.

He was too busy learning the tricks of the trade to learn the trade.

He has a rare gift of instant decision that's heading his firm for bankruptcy.

Two big firms are fighting for his services. The loser gets him.

He's as necessary as a fence around a cemetery.

His furniture is Early American, but it looks more like Late Depression.

He's been dispossessed so many times, he has drapes to match the sidewalk.

Everyone calls him "Arch" because he always needs support.

He's in a hole more often than a gravedigger.

He's always kept his nose to the grindstone, and today he's famous. He's the only person who can cut a steak with his nose.

He's on a merry-go-round—the way of the whirled.

He would have cooked his goose long ago if he had a pot.

Care isn't killing him—it's don't care.

He not only starts things he can't finish; he starts things he can't even begin.

His business is doing as well as a hat-check concession in a nudist colony.

The only way he'll ever make piles of money is to become a bank teller.

He has a difficulty for every solution.

He tried for a corner on the market—now he has a market on the corner.

Everyone speaks highly of him. They say he's perfect—a perfect nonentity.

He has a Phi Beta Kappa key on his watch chain—but no watch.

His business is looking up—it's flat on its back.

He started at the bottom—and stayed there.

He was born with a silver spoon, but never made a stir with it.

He started out with some money and brains, but all he used was the money.

A successful man is game—he's everybody's game.

The only way he'll ever make a name for himself is as a forger.

He's always itching for money, but never scratching for it.

He has as much chance to get anywhere as a guy with a wooden leg in a forest fire.

He bought a retirement policy from his brother-in-law. He kept up his payments for twenty years and his brother-in-law retired.

They call him "Jigsaw." Every time he's faced with a problem, he goes to pieces.

He can always be counted on to hit the nail squarely on the thumb.

The only thing he's ever achieved on his own is dandruff.

He's an early bird who never catches the worm.

He left his home town to set the world on fire. He's going back now for more matches.

He's like a cow that goes dry—udder failure.

They want to pay him what he's worth, but he won't work that cheap.

He left his job because of illness and fatigue—his boss got sick and tired of him.

He was fired with enthusiasm because he wasn't fired with enthusiasm.

He's very well-rounded—too bad he isn't pointed in any direction.

Financially, he's as flat as a rubber doormat.

If he quit work today, he'd have enough to live on for the rest of his life if he died tomorrow.

He's a genius—he can do almost anything except make a living.

He's sliding down the ladder of success so fast, he's getting splinters on his backside.

He's the bustling, rushing, hurrying kind who has never stood still long enough to give life a chance to rub a little sense into him.

The only time he's sure where he's going is when he takes castor oil.

He's always down on something he's not up to—and there's plenty he's not up to.

He had to quit the prize ring because of bad hands—the referee kept stepping on them.

He was knocked out so often, he sold advertising space on the soles of his shoes.

He failed as a druggist—always made his chicken salads too salty.

He's as useful as a pin that has lost its head . . . as a bale of hay in a garage . . . as an umbrella to a hippopotamus . . . as a comb to a baldhead . . . as a fan to an Eskimo . . . as an alarm clock on a Sunday morning . . . as a glass eye at a keyhole . . . as a mustard plaster on a wooden leg . . . as a tire pump in a canoe.

Fair-weather Friends

If you have him for a friend you don't need any enemies.

He sticks with his friends until debt do them part.

He sees that you are through when your real friends see you through.

He's always around—when he needs you.

He picks his friends—to pieces.

He always does his best—including his best friends.

His health is endangered when you lend him money—it damages his memory.

In times of trouble he's waiting to catch you—bent over at the right angle.

If he ever needs a friend, he'll have to buy a dog.

He has friends he hasn't even used yet.

He's a close friend—real close when it comes to helping you out with a loan.

He's a very close friend. Too bad he isn't a generous one.

He'll share your lot with you—if it's a good-sized one.

He claims he's the kind of friend who is hard to find. He's harder to lose.

He has neglected his friends in his drive to make a name for himself. He'd be surprised to know the name they have for him.

He hasn't an enemy in the world and none of his friends like him.

A friend who isn't in need is his friend indeed.

He makes friends fast but never makes fast friends.

He just went out to visit all his friends in the city. He should be back in a few minutes.

You're safe when he holds you tenderly by both hands—because you can watch both of his.

He has perfected the surest way to wipe out a friendship—he sponges on it.

He rolls out the carpet for you one day, and pulls it out from under you the next.

He's only interested in the kind of friends whose inferiority he enjoys.

They tried to get him on the "This Is Your Life" program, but had to give it up. They couldn't find a friend.

You can always depend on him—to depend on you.

He has some very good friends. He never stabs them in the back without a twinge of regret.

You'll always find him on the dock whenever any of his friends' ships come in.

He uses his friendships as a drawing account, but he neglects to make deposits.

The only use he has for a friend is to use him.

He's a real fair-weather friend. He'll always lend you his umbrella on a sunny day.

He's one of those guys who is always close to you until you try to touch him.

He remembers what he gives and forgets what he gets.

He only likes you if you dislike the same people that he dislikes.

In your pursuit of happiness don't expect him to run interference for you.

Fallen Angels

She was very grateful when a fellow gave her that fine undie for her birthday—it was her first slip.

She once let her shoulder-strap slip. It was her first undoing.

She was a pert little thing who went out to flirt and came back ex-pert.

She had no horse sense—she didn't know when to say "Neigh."

She had a slight impediment in her speech—she couldn't say No.

It was soft-soap that made her slip.

She worked on a farm as a milkmaid and the boys gave her a bum steer.

She was a lady's personal maid in a wealthy home. She entered via the servant's entrance and came out in a family way.

She went out on a lark and ended up in a bird's nest.

She's charging the stork with something that should be blamed on a lark.

Apparently she never heard of Mason and Dixon or she might have drawn the line some place.

Her parents didn't worry about her until she was out all night one time, and then it was too late.

They call her the "Baseball Girl" because she was thrown out at home.

It was a country romance. It started out with a pint of corn and ended with a full crib.

Her baby is descended from a long line that she listened to.

She won't see a psychiatrist because a couch is a large part of her trouble.

She sowed wild oats hoping in vain for crop failure.

She drew the line at petting, but he was a football hero so she let him cross the line.

She said she'd do most anything for a fur coat, and when she got it she couldn't button it.

She pursued the wrong policy, so now she needs accident insurance.

Her boy friend's car stalled and she didn't.

She's a brainless beauty who is a toy forever.

She's a dumb girl who didn't turn a deaf ear to a blind date.

She tried to brighten things up for a man by sitting in the dark with him.

Every time the boys take her out, they really take her in.

A fellow offered her a couple of drinks in his apartment and she reclined.

She's more to be petted than censured.

She should have followed the advice "No thyself."

She says the baby's father was deaf and dumb, and by the time she spelled "Stop" out on her fingers it was too late.

At school she was voted the girl most likely to concede.

Her grammar is awful—she can't decline.

She's a Hollywood starlet, and she owes everything to the director who made her.

She collected that expensive wardrobe by starting with a little slip.

She's the kind of pushover you can seduce even if you play your cards wrong.

She goes out with football players but still hasn't learned how to intercept passes.

Everyone calls her "Flour" because she's been through the mill.

She's a May bride—she may be pregnant.

Her trouble started when she got into something light for a heavy date.

Her boy friend is called "Pilgrim" because of the way he makes progress with her.

Her father was so surprised when the fellow said he wanted to marry her, the gun fell right out of his hand.

Her trouble is that the fellows take her with a grain of assault.

A fellow invited her into the woods to hear a nightingale, and it turned out to be a lark.

Features

When she comes into a room, the mice jump on chairs.

She walked into a bar one time, and seven guys took the pledge.

She's good-looking in a way—away off.

She could make a good living renting herself out for Halloween parties.

He's dark and handsome. When it's dark, he's handsome.

He should have been born in the Dark Ages. He sure looks awful in the light.

She looks like a professional blind date.

She looks like a million—every year of it.

Some people can live alone and like it, but she lives alone and looks it.

She loves nature—in spite of what it did to her.

Her boy friend drinks ten cups of coffee a day to steady his nerves so he can look at her.

Her name is Alice, because her German parents took one look at her when she was born, and cried, *"Das ist Alles!"*

The day he was born, his father took one look at him, and ran down to the zoo to throw rocks at the stork.

She could make a good living renting herself out to scare people with the hiccoughs.

Before she introduced him to her family, she told them ghost stories so they wouldn't be scared stiff when they saw him.

A Peeping Tom reached in and pulled down her window shade.

He's the kind you have to look at twice. The first time you don't believe it.

As a bathing beauty, she's hardly worth wading for.

She has the kind of charm that rubs off with a damp cloth.

She looks like a dream—in fact, more like a nightmare.

She has Early American features—she looks like a buffalo.

He looks like an accident going somewhere to happen.

She has everything a man would desire, including heft, bulging muscles, and a moustache.

She has long black hair—and wears long gloves to cover it.

He has as much expression as a smoked herring.

She says she's just back from the beauty parlor—was there two hours. Too bad she wasn't waited on.

She's a vision—a real sight.

There's a good reason why she's been overlooked—she's been looked over.

She'd be safe from advances even if she cooked naked in a lumber camp.

She told a cop, "A man is following me. I think he must be crazy." The cop agreed.

He looks like the first husband of a widow.

At her wedding everybody kissed the groom.

She's the type who thinks it's dishonest to look anything but her worst.

The only thing that can ever make her look good is distance.

Once she asked her husband, "Look me right in the face." He answered, "I can't. I've got my own problems."

She's becoming an operating-room nurse because she's better off wearing a mask.

If that isn't her face, how come it looks like it's done up in curlers?

Once, having lost her wrist watch, she accurately advertised: "Lost, wrist watch by a lady with a cracked face."

She's had so many face-lifting jobs, every time she raises her eyebrows, she pulls up her stockings.

She's had her face lifted so many times, it's out of focus.

She's all dressed up and no face to go.

He has a face you don't want to remember and can't forget.

She has a face that looks like it wore out six bodies.

He has a face like a saint—a Saint Bernard.

Her face isn't her fortune—it's her chaperone.

She has a winning smile and a losing face.

He has the kind of a map only Rand McNally could love.

Only an auctioneer would be pleased with her face—it's forbidding.

You can't blame her for lying about her face, now that her face is being truthful about it.

You have a very striking face. How many times have you been struck there?

If I had your face, I'd hire a pickpocket to lift it.

I recall your name all right, but I just can't think of your face.

She has the kind of a face that once seen is never remembered.

She's had her face lifted so many times there's nothing left inside her shoes.

If Moses had seen *his* face, there would have been another commandment.

She looks like she just stepped out of *Vogue*, and fell flat on her face.

She's not really two-faced. If she had two, why would she be wearing that one?

I never forget a face, but with yours I'll make an exception.

A kind man said to her, "When I look at you, time stands still." What he really meant was that her face would stop a clock.

He has a face that really grows on people. But if it grew on them, they'd chop it off.

Is that your face, or did you block a kick?

At bedtime, her face is as greased as an English Channel swimmer's.

Her photographs do her an injustice—they look like her.

It hasn't helped her to have her face lifted, so she's thinking of lowering her body instead.

Two weeks ago she put mud on her face to improve her looks. It improved her looks so much, she hasn't taken it off yet.

The only way he can get some color in his face is to stick his tongue out.

She packs so much mud on her face at bedtime, her husband would be at home if he was lost in a swamp.

He has a fairly good nose, as noses run.

He can't run for President. They couldn't get his nose on a stamp.

Her nostrils are so big, when you kiss her it's like driving into a two-car garage.

Is that your nose—or are you eating a banana?

He can overlook everything—except his nose.

She has a nice chin, and for her mother that goes double.

She has two chins, going on three.

He could go through life taking it on the chin if he knew which one it was.

He would have been a great violinist, but he couldn't figure out which chin to put the fiddle under.

She has stopped patting herself on the back and started patting herself under the chin.

His lower jaw recedes so much, he has to use his Adam's apple for a chin.

He has so many cavities in his teeth. he talks with an echo.

Her teeth are like pearls—they need stringing.

Her teeth are so far apart, every time she opens her mouth she looks like a picket fence.

He has only three teeth, and one of them he got when he joined the Elks.

She has two beautiful eyes. Too bad they're not mates.

The way she keeps her eyebrows it certainly takes a lot of pluck.

She lost her job as a cook. She's so cockeyed, the folks never knew where their next meal was coming from.

He has watchman's eyes. They both keep watching his nose.

He's a store detective. He's so cross-eyed, nobody knows whom he's watching.

He's so nearsighted, he once lost a bass fiddle in a one-room apartment.

He was turned down for an operator's license on account of nearsightedness—he had his wife along.

He's as nearsighted as a mole.

He sleeps quite comfortably—he has such big pillows under his eyes.

When she cries, the tears from her right eye fall on her left cheek.

She has dyed by her own hand.

They call her "Kitty" because she has dyed nine times.

She's a cross between a brunette and a drugstore.

Some women are blond on their mother's side, some on their father's side, but she's blond on the peroxide.

She's an established bleachhead.

There's one trouble with her upsweep hair-do. It's hard to tell where she swept it up from.

With that hair-do, it's like looking for a noodle in a haystack to find her.

At the movies, they have to ask her to take off her hair.

She has one of those new hair tints—hue-it-yourself.

As a blonde, she's chemistry's greatest contribution to the world.

She's showing her true colors. She hasn't been to the hairdresser's for three weeks.

Was she embarrassed when she was asked to remove her mask at the masquerade party! She didn't have one on.

Her wrinkles are all where her smiles should have been.

She has enough wrinkles in her face to hold a three-day rain.

She has more wrinkles than a dried plum.

He's a man of polish—mostly around his head.

He combs his hair with a sponge.

He sure has blown his top.

He has less hair to comb, but more face to wash.

It's not that he's bald-headed—he just has a tall face.

Get a load of that head of skin.

He gets less for his money every time he goes to the barber.

His mouth is so big, he can eat a banana sideways.

He has something to snicker at every day—he shaves daily.

He has such a receding chin, he has no trouble eating corn on the cob.

Figures

She's losing her girlish figure and her boyish husband.

She not only has kept her girlish figure—she has doubled it.

She has a Supreme Court figure—no appeal.

She's pretty well reared. She doesn't look so good in front either.

Now that her husband is rich enough to buy her dresses for a fancy figure, she no longer has one.

Not only isn't her face her fortune, but the other parts don't draw interest either.

She doesn't have the figure for a bikini—just the nerve.

She boasts she got that dress for a ridiculous figure. Obviously.

She's far from her old sylph.

Anatomy is something every woman has, but on her it doesn't look so good.

She has a figure like an hourglass. It takes an hour to figure out what it is.

The only way she could cut quite a figure is by sitting down on a broken bottle.

Too bad she isn't as well-formed as she is well-informed.

She's too lazy to watch her figure, so the boys don't either.

The fellows look up to her rather than around.

The only thing that saves her from being figureless is her Adam's apple.

He's in the punk of condition.

He's so anemic, he has to get a transfusion in order to bleed.

He's so anemic, the only way he can get any color in his face is to stick his tongue out.

He's so emaciated, if he were alive he'd be a very sick man.

He can get a $200 advance from any undertaker.

The shape he's in, his insurance agent is demanding his calendar and blotters back.

It's lucky for him he's not a building or he'd be condemned.

With those varicose veins, she could win first prize at a costume party by going as a road map.

He retired after twenty-five years of service—he received a silver ulcer.

I wouldn't say his condition's critical, but I wouldn't advise him to start a magazine serial.

He has such high blood pressure, if it wasn't for his skin he'd be a fountain.

He's the cave-man type—one hug and he caves in.

He's as flabby as a sponge.

He has such a bad case of insomnia, the sheep are picketing him for shorter hours.

He doesn't sleep because of worry—worry about not sleeping.

He suffers from insomnia worse than a bedbug.

Even when he sleeps, he dreams he doesn't.

He's so thin, his muscles look like flea bites on a piece of spaghetti.

She's as thin as a whisper.

He can make a good living doing scarecrow work.

The only thing a sweater does for her is keep her warm.

She's so thin, she could walk through a harp.

He's getting so thin, the watermelon he had tattooed on his chest looks like an olive now.

She's so thin, she can take a bath in a fountain pen.

Every time she yawns, her dress falls down.

She has an income tax figure. The Internal Revenue is after her for not filling out her form.

She's so thin, she doesn't have enough on her to itch.

You have to look at her twice to see her once.

When her husband takes her to a restaurant, the headwaiter asks him to check his umbrella.

A real estate man jilted her because of her unattractive frontage.

They call her "Seven-Eleven" because when she walks you can hear her bones rattle.

She recently swallowed an olive and was rushed to a maternity hospital.

She has to pass a place twice to cast a shadow.

He has an outstanding personality. It's centered in his bay window.

She's a perfect model—for a shipbuilder.

It would do her good to practice girth control.

She has to put on a girdle to get into a kimono.

His opulence is only exceeded by his corpulence.

If he ever gets into an elevator it had better be going down.

He has an easygoing nature. He's too heavy to run and too fat to fight.

He's living way beyond his seams.

The only thing about him that's getting thinner is his hair.

He's so fat, when he falls down he rocks himself to sleep trying to get up.

He used to be spic and span, but now he's more span than spic.

I knew him when he had only one stomach and one chin.

He's too fat to play golf. If he puts the ball where he can hit it, he can't see it, and if he puts it where he can see it, he can't hit it.

The way he eats, no wonder he gets thick to his stomach.

Success has brought him not only poise but avoirdupois.

The lines of her body are the lines of real resistance.

The way she overeats she'll never break the pound barrier.

She can eat anything and never gain a pound—over 175.

She's the living proof that you can't eat your cake and have "It."

She's living in a food's paradise that is fast putting an end to her.

When it comes to her wearing slacks, the end doesn't justify the jeans.

The only way she reigns superior is with her jutting posterior.

The way she's putting on weight, she'll never be her old sylph again.

The trouble with her is she's not sylph-conscious.

With all that food going to waist, she's a real hippochondriac.

It wouldn't hurt her to go to some length to change her width.

The trouble with the bulk of women like her is where it shows.

She keeps forgetting that a moment on the lips is a lifetime on the hips.

She's one of those women who eat too much sweets and have too much seats.

She'll never realize woman's fondest wish—to be weighed and found wanting.

She was recently on a strict diet—all she lost was her temper.

When she wears slacks she reveals stern facts.

She claims she lost five pounds but she should take a look behind her.

Her bathing suits let her swim but not slink.

The photographer couldn't show her most outstanding side. She was sitting on it.

She's enlarging not only her sphere but her circumference.

She sure stretches the truth when she wears those tight ski pants.

Her obesity is a matter of just deserts—only a bulge in a girdled cage.

Her obesity is surplus gone to waist.

Her waistline is definitely of her own chewsing.

She weighs one hundred and plenty.

She's no good at all at counting calories and she has the figure to prove it.

She's one of the five million overweight women. These, of course, are round figures.

All the exercise he ever gets is moving food from the plate to the palate.

His idea of interior decoration is an enormous meal.

He lives by dinner time instead of inner time.

He must be eating army food. Everything he eats goes to the front.

His wife got rid of 235 pounds of ugly fat—she divorced him.

When it comes to food, he's all will and a yard wide.

He has no trouble at all watching his waistline—it's right there in front where he can see it.

On account of his unrestrainable appetite, everyone is having fun at his expanse.

He might lose some weight if he kept his mouth and the refrigerator closed.

His doctor put him on a seven-day diet, but he ate the whole thing in one meal.

He'll eat anything that won't bite first.

The way she indulges explains her bulges, and she can blame the platter as she gets fatter.

That cheese cake she likes so much is fast turning into pound cake.

It's a crime the way she overeats; her girdle is the punishment that fits the crime.

She eats so much, no wonder her shape is like a figure ate.

Her clothes are designed to make her look younger, but she'll never fool a flight of stairs.

She has lost in youth what she has won in weight.

She has a real shady background. She has hips like a beach umbrella.

She has switchboard hips—every line is busy.

She has a figure like a pillow.

He's so fat in shorts, he looks like a chiffonier—a big thing with drawers.

He's so fat, his wife gave him a belt for Christmas and he's using it for a wrist watch.

He's so paunchy, his wife would like him better the more she saw him less.

The only good thing you can say for his obesity is that a great deal of him is having a good time.

Her figure reveals that she could help herself more by helping herself to less.

The only well-rounded thing about her is her figure.

She's like a foreign car—she has all her weight in the rear.

Her figure indicates a need for exercise—like shaking her head from side to side when offered a second helping.

She'd do well to follow that fine slenderizing advice: "Don't chew—eschew."

It would do her good to go to the beach. Last year's bathing suit will induce her to go out of her weigh to be slimmer.

Flat Tires

Some women get orchids—all she gets are forget-me-notes.

Girls return his letters marked "Fourth Class Male."

She hasn't a gent to her name.

She's not fussy. If she can't get a man 6 foot 3, she settles for one 3 foot 6.

She'll never be the center of Ah-traction.

He sent his picture to the Lonely Hearts Club. The reply came back, "We're not that lonely."

He always looks as uncomfortable as a centipede with athlete's foot.

She's so unattractive, when the boss chases her around the desk, he walks.

She's two-thirds married—she's willing and so is her mother.

She's working like a horse to get a groom.

When she swears she's never been kissed, you can't blame her for swearing.

His idea of an exciting night is to turn up his electric blanket.

When he hears a girl singing in the bathtub, he puts his ear to the keyhole.

If he took up burglary, he couldn't even steal a kiss from an old maid.

He could get lost in a crowd of two.

She's studying to be a contortionist so she can sit in her own lap.

The only man she ever had at her feet was a chiropodist.

The only time she's ever squeezed is when she wears tight shoes and girdles.

She's such a wallflower, she comes home wearing the same lipstick she started out with.

After the boys look her over, they overlook her.

She dated him because he was an old flame, but he turned out to be a silly ash.

He's a real Don Juan with women—they *Don Juan* to have anything to do with him.

He's the type who talks astronomy to a luscious blonde on a moonlit night.

He's a real nature lover—he goes into the woods at night without a girl.

The only time he ever raves about nylon stockings is when they're empty.

Until you've met him, you're sure that the largest prune is six inches in diameter.

He has the personality of the back wall of a handball court.

He was the life of the party. This gives you an idea of how dull the party was.

His life is so dull, he actually looks forward to dental appointments.

He's the kind you ask to stay with you when you want to be alone.

He went out for football, because when he was born his parents took one look at him and shouted, "That's the end."

The fellows wind her up but she doesn't spin.

She has as much sex appeal as a bedtime story over the radio.

Her parents warned her that life is full of temptations, but so far no one has tempted her.

She hasn't had mush experience.

She's smart—a regular encyclopedia. One thing she doesn't know—reference books are never taken out.

Life for her has been a hit-or-miss proposition. She doesn't make a hit, so she remains a miss.

She's as lonesome as a bachelor's toothbrush.

She's been engaged to some promising men—too bad they didn't keep their promises.

Landing a man on the moon doesn't worry her nearly as much as landing one right here on earth.

She has decided to be an airline hostess—it's the only job where she can strap a man down.

Oh, the youthlessness of her existence!

She knows all the answers but nobody asks her the question.

If she found a man in her bedroom, she'd give him twenty-four hours to get out.

She could have married any man she pleased. Trouble was, she never pleased one.

Given the choice of a man with brains, money, or appearance, she would unquestionably pick appearance—and the sooner the better.

She's unhappily unmarried.

She went to college for four years—and whom did it get her?

She's an unemployed schoolteacher—she has no class.

She'll die quite happily; she just heard that marriages are made in heaven.

They call her "Dusty" because she's been on the shelf so long.

They call her "Checkers" because she jumps when the boys make a wrong move.

They call her "Lily" because she likes to go out with dead ones.

They call her "Appendix"—if you take her out once, that's enough.

They call her "Poison Ivy" because she's an awful thing to have on your hands.

Goat-Getters

He's a pain in the neck, and some people have even a lower opinion of him.

He thinks the world is against him. What's more, he's right.

The more you think of him the less you think of him.

When you first meet him, you don't like him; but after you get to know him better, you detest him.

When he was born, something terrible happened—he lived.

He's called a big thinker—by people who lisp.

He's a buried treasure. Too bad they dug him up.

When he was a child, his parents almost lost him; but they didn't take him far enough out in the woods.

Everyone has as much use for him as a duck for a life preserver.

He makes you wish birth control could be made retroactive.

He's not only a bachelor—he's a bachelor's son.

There's something about him that definitely attracts women —to other men.

Man is said to be only a little lower than the angels. If he's an example, they'd better start checking on the angels.

Someone once told him to be himself. He couldn't have been given worse advice.

We all spring from monkeys, but he didn't spring far enough.

He descends from the early Boons. His ancestors were Baboons.

He does serve at least one useful purpose in life—as a horrible example.

He lacks only a few more obnoxious traits to be perfect.

It's not the ups and downs in life that bother the average person; it's the jerks—like him.

Lots of people would enjoy working for him—gravediggers, for instance.

He may be a tonic to his family—he's a pill to everyone else.

He acts that way because he's repressed. In his youth, his mother slapped him—because he set fire to his grandmother.

He's mean, selfish, loudmouthed, and uncouth, but in spite of all that, there's something about him that repels you.

He's high-strung, but not nearly high enough.

He was born in the United States. Terrible things happen in other countries too.

His staff threw him a big dinner. Unfortunately, it didn't hit him.

He doesn't have an enemy. All his friends hate him.

He has a fine personality—but not for a human being.

If he ever finds himself out, he's not going to like it.

He has very winning ways—to make himself disliked.

Everyone calls him "Webster." Words can't describe him.

He once asked a girl if she could learn to love a guy like him, and she answered, "Yes, if he isn't too much like you."

It's not his money that counts. People just hate him for himself alone.

It wouldn't do him a bit of good to see himself as others see him. He wouldn't believe it.

He was a premature baby. He was born before his parents were married.

He hasn't been himself lately. Everyone wishes he would stay that way.

His parents never struck him, except in self-defense.

There's nothing wrong with him that reincarnation won't cure.

Even if he spent $1,000 on a halitosis cure, no one would like him anyway.

He's like a male baby bee—a son of a bee.

Someday he's going to go too far, and everyone hopes he'll stay there.

His family and friends don't mind if he smokes. In fact, they don't mind if he burns.

He hasn't many faults, but he sure makes the most of the ones he has.

Everyone has the right to have some faults, but he abuses the privilege.

Nobody has a higher opinion of him than his closest friends; they think he's a first-class louse.

They're speaking well of him lately—he must be dead.

He's just what the doctor ordered—a pill.

If he could only see himself as others see him, he'd never speak to them again.

He's marrying a female X-ray specialist. No one else can see anything in him.

He has one very highly developed instinct—for being obnoxious.

He's not really his own worst enemy—not while anyone who has anything to do with him is still living.

It's useless to ask him to act like a human being. He doesn't do imitations.

He'll improve himself when crows turn white.

He's a genius. He not only takes infinite pains with what he's doing—he gives them.

He hates the human race. That's because he thinks he's as good as anybody, and he's repulsive.

He'll leave everything to his heirs—except regrets.

He once belonged to a fife-and-drum corps. They kicked him out because he was rotten to the corps.

Some day he's going to need a friend, and he's going to find it hard to get one.

He's very fastidious—fast and hideous.

You can always count on him to display his pest manners.

Someone ought to rent him out to a near-sighted knife-thrower.

His country club is having a membership drive next week—they're going to drive him out.

He's so unpopular, he's developing B.O. to attract attention.

Most of his remarks belong in the dead-letter office—they're uncalled for.

At first people don't care much for him; but he grows on them—the little wart.

His folks didn't know the meaning of "quit" until he was born.

He was left $50,000 in the will of a woman he once jilted—a case of real, heartfelt gratitude.

Years pass, but he doesn't—more's the pity.

Life is what you make it—until he comes around and makes it worse.

His mother-in-law calls him "Son," but she never completes the sentence.

Gold Diggers

So far as men are concerned, she can take them or leave them. After she takes them, she leaves them.

She has a million-dollar smile. She only smiles at guys with a million dollars.

Her motto is: "Dough or die."

She buys spring clothes in the middle of the winter for summer romances with fall guys.

The only man she'll go out with is one who is tall, dark, and has some.

Men of means are worth her wiles.

She spells "Matrimony" "Matter-o' money."

The only love nest she's interested in is an eight-room apartment feathered with cash down.

She's always ready to go out for a little fund.

She doesn't mind whose means she lives beyond.

When it comes to men she prefers the strong, solvent type.

It's hard to figure what she would have found attractive about men if she had lived before money was invented.

It's not too difficult to find her. Just open your wallet, and there she is!

She's climbing the ladder of success lad by lad and wrong by wrong.

She's the cream in a guy's coffee as long as he has plenty of sugar.

She's getting along fine—by lips and bonds.

A guy never knows the worth of her love until she sues him for breach of promise.

Her motto is: Think—Mink!

She's looking for a rich guy to make her dreams come through.

She's a good listener—when money talks.

She may get married someday. She's just waiting for the right amount to come along.

In her estimation, a man doesn't have to *be* much if he has much.

All she looks for in a man is brown eyes and green money.

She brings out the animal in men—Mink.

What she looks for in a man is fiscal fitness.

She knows how to stay in the mink of condition.

She doesn't believe in love blindfolded—she wants it billfolded.

Her hobby is collecting romantic antiques—rich old geezers.

Men call her "Sugar" and wind up paying her a lump sum.

She meets a wolf at the door and appears next day in a fur coat.

She'll go out with every Tom, Dick, and Harry, provided they bring jack along.

She sure knows how to mine her own business, especially where diamonds are concerned.

A fellow starts out by calling her "Sugar" and winds up a sad saccharine.

She prefers men who have something tender about them—legal tender.

She's looking for a generous man—one she can take to, and from.

She hails from the corn belt, but all she's interested in now is the money belt.

She gets a grand and glorious feeling when a fellow makes love to her—especially a grand.

When money stops talking, she starts walking.

She falls in love at purse sight.

She speaks only in moneysyllables.

Some girls keep their love letters, but she lets the love letters keep her.

The only thing she's ever been taken in by is a girdle.

She takes everything that a guy can buy; then she takes another guy.

A fellow's love letters are her jilt-edge securities.

She's the one exception to the law of gravity. It's easier to pick her up than to drop her.

Some girls frame the first dollar they ever made. She framed the first man.

If you spoon around with her you have to fork over.

She gets her mink by being like a fox and playing cat-and-mouse with a wolf.

She gets her men by using her come-on sense.

She's a vegetarian. She only goes out with men with plenty of lettuce.

She measures a man's love by the carat.

She loves a man for all he's worth—after he passes the assets test.

Whenever she sued for breach of promise she was calm—and collected.

She dresses on credit, but she'll only undress for cash.

She defrauds the males by using them.

A fellow said he would go through anything for her, so she started right off with his bank account.

She's going out with a sugar daddy. He met her thirty-five checks ago.

Her motto is: "Every man for myself."

She may be good for nothing, but she's never bad for nothing.

She has a great talent for womaneuvers.

Her favorite book is Dun and Bradstreet.

She's a human gimme-pig.

When she threatens to tell a guy's wife, the furs really fly.

Her crowning glory is a rich guy's scalp.

She loves everything about America—the people of America, the songs of America, the Bank of America.

When she gives you that baby stare, you're safer in the electric chair.

She's a female wolf in chic clothing.

She's as true as steel—provided it's U. S. Steel.

Her beautiful eyes have put many a man on the blink.

She pulls the wool over men's eyes, by wearing sweaters that pull their eyes over the wool.

It's the little things about a husband that she likes, like small penthouses, small yachts, small racing stables, and small life expectancies.

She's interested in do-re-mi and she's going fa'.

She started out with a full knowledge about the birds and bees—and she learned fast about the minks.

She likes a guy whose conversation sparkles—with things like emeralds, rubies, diamonds, and sapphires.

She sure has the gift of grab.

She never sells herself for cash—she takes checks, stocks, bonds, and shares in oil wells.

Magic is her hobby—like getting mink off an old goat.

Around town they call her "Cinderella"—the fellows have to slipper fifty, slipper a hundred.

She paints the town red with a guy with a bankroll—she gives him the brush when it's gone.

She's one tomato who knows her onions. She knows how to get guys with lots of lettuce.

It doesn't take long to find there's method in her badness.

She once married a guy for money. She divorced him for the same reason.

Once she gets a guy on the spot, she takes him to the cleaners.

She's sure she has the right dope, that her latest boy friend makes $25,000 a year—at least until a better dope comes along.

She worships the ground where her Texas boy friend discovered oil.

She prefers men who go in for the refined things in life—like oil.

It's the thought—not the gift—that counts with her and the bigger it is the more it counts.

She never kisses a man with beer on his breath—it has to be champagne.

She had a hard row to hoe, so she got an old rake to make it easier for her.

She's working at loving—for a living.

She's great at getting not only the seal of a man's approval, but the mink as well.

She doesn't offer much resistance, so she leads a very nice existence.

She even purses her lips when she's kissed.

She's a great after-dinner speaker. When she speaks to a man, she's after a dinner.

She's always trying to break her boy friends of a bad habit—eating alone.

She's looking for a man with a green thumb—green from peeling off hundred-dollar bills.

She always has lots of men on her arm, but none in her heart.

She has been tried and found wanting—everything money can buy her.

After a guy has spent all his dollars, she recovers her sense.

She loves a man for his money up to a certain point—the decimal point.

She doesn't mind men who love her and leave her, provided they leave her enough.

She doesn't mind if a man doesn't fit the bill so long as he foots it.

She knows how to write letters that speed up the males.

She's looking for a rich man who wants to take her away from it all. Then she'll take it all away from him.

Her idea of a steppingstone to success is a 20-carat stone.

Her concern is not so much what a man stands for as what he falls for.

She doesn't look for too much in a man—just someone to spend with the rest of her life.

She met a man who had more money than he knew what to do with. Now she has it—and he's had it.

She knows how to make feminine capital out of masculine interest.

Her men friends think they're being cultivated, but they're being trimmed.

She'll never be happy until she meets John Dough.

She's a human dynamo. She charges everything—to her sugar daddies.

If a guy takes her for two weeks on the sands, he's sure to spend the next fifty weeks on the rocks.

She couldn't decide what to give a guy who had already given her everything, so she gave him the air.

Her resistance at the start is not so much a proof of her virtue as her experience.

She took her last three husbands not for better or worse, but for good.

There isn't a man who can pin anything on her—not made of diamonds, or hang anything on her—not made of pearls.

Gossips

Tell her a secret, and she's sure to chin and bare it.

She's always letting the chat out of the bag.

His business is what's none of his business.

Anything you tell her goes in one ear and over the back fence.

She's a slight-of-tongue artist.

Her gossip is strictly her-say.

She dotes on cocktail parties where sandwiches and acquaintances are cut into little pieces.

She has a tongue that could clip a hedge.

Wind him up and he's sure to run someone down.

She picks up more dirt with the telephone than she does with the vacuum cleaner.

He has passed from his formative to his informative years.

He likes to be first with the worst.

She's known as "Dame Gossip"—and some folks omit the "e."

There are three quick ways of spreading news: telephone, telegraph, and tell-her.

He can sling dirt faster than a gravedigger.

She burns her scandals at both ends.

He's on spiking terms with everyone.

Her tongue is her sword, and she makes sure it never gets rusty.

He's the type of eavesdropper who gets in your hear.

She clucks like a hen over her grains of gossip.

A good description of her would be fair to meddling.

She never repeats gossip—she's always the one who starts it.

She has a keen sense of rumor.

She doesn't know certain people well enough to talk to, but well enough to talk about.

In a beauty parlor, her gossip alone can curl your hair.

She joined a sewing circle—it was the ideal place to needle everyone.

Keeping a secret from her is like trying to sneak daybreak past a rooster.

With her, a rumor goes in one ear, and out through her mouth.

He's an expert in hintimation.

He has more inside information than a surgeon.

They call him "Stretch" because he has an elastic conscience and a rubber neck.

Automobiles don't run down as many people as he does.

Her motto is: "One touch of scandal makes the whole world chin."

She's the vacuum-cleaner type—she purrs and takes in the dirt.

Most of the rumors he spreads are over the sour grapevine.

She listens in haste and repeats at leisure.

She'll gladly listen to both sides of an argument—if it's her neighbors, talking on a party line.

She has a way of saying nothing that leaves practically nothing unsaid.

He'll never tell a lie—when the truth will do more damage.

He thinks he's polished because everything he says casts a reflection on someone.

She has a good memory, and a tongue hung in the middle of it.

She's such a busybody, she had her appendix removed so she could see what it looked like.

She constantly goes to an ear specialist to prevent over-hearing trouble.

She can keep a secret—with telling effect.

Her plastic surgeon was able to do everything with her nose except keep it out of other people's business.

She's terrific at putting one and one together—to make talk.

He's a sociologist on a petty scale; he's always pouring social sewerage into people's ears.

He's the knife of the party.

You can always depend on him to give you the benefit of the dirt.

If one half of the world doesn't know how the other half lives, it isn't his fault.

He doesn't knock before he enters your home, but he knocks plenty after he leaves it.

Her tongue hangs out like a pump handle.

She's suffering from acute indiscretion.

She's as inquisitive as an X-ray.

She has the words of a saint and the claws of a cat.

She seldom repeats gossip—the way she heard it.

She always talks about things that she says left her speechless.

She just can't leave bad enough alone.

She's unhappiest when every member of her women's club shows up.

They call her "Olive"—the way she sticks her nose in other people's business.

She detests gossip—but only when it's about herself.

Her acquaintances may not be the best informed people, but they certainly are the most informed.

Her gossip is an ill wind that blows nobody good.

Her tongue is like a pink dart.

Husbands
(Henpecked)

He brags that he's the boss in his home, but he lies about other things too.

She leads a double life—hers and his.

When she wants his opinion, she gives it to him.

He wears the pants in the house—under his apron.

He comes right out and says what she tells him to think.

They are two minds with but a single thought—hers.

He has been married twenty awed years.

Everything he owns is hers—especially his nerve.

He has the courage of her convictions.

He has two chances of winning an argument with her—slim and none.

She has her way when they agree, and he has her way when they disagree.

She doesn't have to raise the roof. All she has to do is raise an eyebrow.

Whenever he has a contented look on his face, she wipes it off with a dish towel.

The only time he opens his mouth is to ask her for the apron and the vacuum cleaner.

He doesn't snore in his sleep—he cackles.

He always has the last word—he says, "I apologize."

She snaps, "Are you a man or a mouse—squeak up!"

He was a man-about-town, but she turned him into a mouse-around-the-house.

The last big decision she let him make was whether to wash or dry.

She tames to be pleased.

She lost her thumb in an accident and sued for $100,000, because it was the thumb she had him under.

She jumps when he speaks—all over him.

He's very cooperative—he washes up when asked and dries up when told.

He's grateful to be living in a free country where a man can do as his wife pleases.

She's his solace, but if it wasn't for her he wouldn't need any solace.

He put a ring on her finger and she put one through his nose.

She always forgives him when she's in the wrong.

He's her altered ego.

She's his booin' companion.

He can't even open his mouth to yawn—she complains it causes a draft.

He married her for her looks, but not the kind he's getting now.

He was a dude before marriage—now he's subdued.

He even has to ask permission to ask permission.

His parakeet gets to talk more than he does.

She even complains about the noise he makes fixing his own breakfast.

They had a big difference of opinion about getting a dishwasher. She says he doesn't need one.

He goes to a woman dentist. It's a relief to be told to open his mouth instead of shut it.

On an application blank asking his marital status, he wrote, "Below wife."

He worships the ground she gives him the run-around on.

He has his will, but she has her way.

He's definitely not a yes-man. When she says No, he says No.

He's a man of strong determination. Whenever he makes up his mind to tell her to do something, *he* does it.

He gave her an inch and now she's the ruler.

They had a very amusing argument recently. When she threw the axe at him, he thought he'd split.

He walks with his head high and erect—he has a stiff neck.

Once he complained, "You're driving me to my grave." In a minute, she had the car in front of the house.

When he's late for dinner, he gets two kinds of meat—hot tongue and cold shoulder.

He should have been warned, when he carried her over the threshold after they were married, that she couldn't wait to put her foot down.

He should have known he was in for it when right after they were married she took charge of the electric blanket controls.

He should have caught wise at the altar. When he said, "I do," she snapped, "No, you don't."

Every once in awhile she comes to him on her bended knees. She dares him to come out from under the bed.

He keeps his teeth in perfect condition—he doesn't argue with her.

He holds his pay envelope up to the light to see if he got a raise.

They've been married five years and she still hasn't told him how much money he's earning.

She instructed his firm's paymaster to mail his check home and eliminate the middleman.

She denies he's henpecked. She sometimes gives him permission to smoke a big black cigar while he washes the dishes.

He spends his evenings solving crossword puzzles—she hands him the cross words.

He never argues with her. He might win—and then he'd really be in trouble.

It's a mutual partnership—he's the mute.

His name is Alexander, but in his home he's Alexander the

Great. Whenever the furnace gets low, she hollers, "Alexander! the grate."

She wants to go to the seashore, claiming that mountain air disagrees with her. He can't see how it would dare.

It doesn't take much to make her purr like a kitten. All he has to do is rub her the right way.

Despite the statistics, he denies that married men live longer than single men—it only seems longer.

He says he runs his house like a ship, with him as the captain. The only trouble is, she's the admiral.

It's his second marriage, and now he has a new leash on life.

She's very thoughtful. She asks him what he would like for dinner—then she picks out a restaurant that serves it.

In a restaurant, out of force of habit, she makes him help the waiter with the dishes.

When she suggests going out to eat, he says forcefully, "We're not going to a restaurant—and that's semifinal."

In their home, she's the chairman of the ways-and-mean-it committee.

He's a very tender husband. No wonder. She always keeps him in hot water.

He's a very agreeable husband—he's always agreeing with her.

He's very forceful—he can make her do anything she wants to do.

He wishes Adam had died with all his ribs in his body.

They always compromise. He admits he's wrong and she forgives him.

The story of his courtship and marriage: He came, he saw, he concurred.

When he asks her to darn his socks, she knits her brow.

She not only wears the pants in the family, she wears the whole suit.

He never knows when he's well off because he never is.

When she takes him to the supermarket, he looks exactly like a man being led to the shopping block.

She always reminds him that he can be replaced, now that machines are being developed that respond to spoken commands.

She uses a very efficient weed-killer in the garden—him.

Their marriage is harmonious so long as he plays second fiddle.

This guy is really henpecked. She even makes him wash and iron his own aprons.

For Easter, she gave him a rabbit punch.

He has a soft spot in his head for her.

The only time she runs her fingers through his hair is when she can't find the towel.

When the traffic cop asked him if he got the number of the hit-and-run driver who had bowled him over, he said, "No, but I'd recognize my wife's laugh anywhere."

It's a perfect love match. He loves her and so does she.

It would be nice if she thought more *of* him than *for* him.

She's made a lasting impression on him. The doctor says the scars will never disappear.

He's the Sovereign, Unconquerable, Supreme, Grand Potentate of his lodge, but he's missed three meetings because she won't let him go.

She telephoned a friend, "I have marvelous news—what a break! My husband had a heart attack and we have to go to Florida for the winter."

He married her to have someone to tell his troubles to, and now he certainly has plenty to talk about.

She's all preaches and scream.

She's a real womanacle.

He's real spousebroken.

Husbands
(The Bitter Half)

They were married for better or for worse. He couldn't have done better and she couldn't have done worse.

Whoever said women can't take a joke evidently hasn't seen the specimen she married.

It was love at first sight. She should have wiped her glasses for a second look.

It must have been love at first sight. If she had taken a second look, she'd have turned and run.

She must have had a real open mind to fall in love with him —a big hole in the head.

It's her second marriage, and now she has a new louse on life.

All she's gotten out of their marriage is bed and boredom.

It's a trial marriage—nothing could be more of a trial.

She has a fine prospect of happiness behind her.

It's not at all true that everyone has a sane spot somewhere—wait till you meet him.

She'll never forget the first time they met, but she's trying hard.

She married him to reform him, and then found that the rites didn't right him and the altar didn't alter him.

He was her ideal before marriage—now he's an ordeal.

She married him for his money, and she's earning every dollar of it.

The only reason she's had nine children by him is that she's trying to lose him in a crowd.

Just before his birthday, her friends asked what she was getting for him, and she said, "Make me an offer."

He's made her so nervous she's losing weight, but she won't leave him. She's waiting till he gets her down to 125 pounds.

Their marriage is like baking bread. She's got plenty of dough and he's got plenty of crust.

He married her for her money, and he's giving her everything her money can buy.

He's a go-getter. His wife has a lucrative job, and on payday he makes sure to go get 'er.

He lives by the sweat of his frau.

She married a dreamer, and found he's just a sleeper.

She thought she was getting a model husband—but he's not a working model.

He has a certain something, but she wishes he had something certain.

He isn't a self-starter, so she's become a crank.

She's the driving force in the household, so he bought her a hammer and nails.

He steadies the stepladder for her while she paints the kitchen ceiling.

He likes to mow the lawn in the winter and shovel snow in the summer.

She banks her hard-earned dollars, while he deposits his quarters in an easy chair.

The only exercise he gets is prying frozen ice trays out of the refrigerator.

Although he loafs half the time, she hasn't left him. She feels half a loafer is better than none.

He boasts that he never made a mistake—but he has a wife who did.

She avoids getting up with a grouch—she rises before he does.

When she asks him a question, she has to take a lot for grunted.

He takes his troubles like a man—he blames them on her.

She says he doesn't carry life insurance, just fire insurance —he knows where he's going.

When she accuses him of being a cross, grouchy, ill-mannered brute, he wheedles, "Look, honey, you know no man's perfect."

He needed a wife because sooner or later something was bound to happen that he couldn't blame on the government.

"You say you loved me," she tells him. "If you really did, why didn't you marry someone else?"

The gift she'd appreciate most is something he made himself—like money.

When she asks him for clothes money, he tells her to "go to the best shops and pick some nice things—but don't get caught."

She didn't realize when she sank into his arms, that she would wind up with her arms in the sink.

He promised her a convertible after they were married and he's kept his promise. She's wheeling a baby carriage with the top down.

She wanted a mink coat, so he got her a trap and a gun.

She's demanding a harness. If she works like a horse, she wants to look like a horse.

He treats the money he gives her like horse-radish—he parts with it with tears in his eyes.

He hates to see a woman in cheap clothes—unless, of course, she's his wife.

She bought him underwear initialed B.V.D, and he shot a neighbor whose name was Bernard V. Donaldson.

When he saw the twins for the first time, he insisted that one looked like the milkman and the other like the plumber.

He threatens to divorce her because she said she loved him more than anybody else in the world; that proved to him she was experimenting.

He's studying to be a trapeze artist so he can catch her in the act.

She keeps saying, "Tell me again what a good married life we're having—I keep forgetting."

He's supporting her in the manner to which she was accustomed—he's letting her keep her job.

He called her his cute little dish—now she's his cute little dishwasher.

The doctor says she needs sea air, so he's fanning her with a mackerel.

A fortuneteller told her she'd be a widow soon—that her husband would die by poisoning—and she asked, "Will I be acquitted?"

All she wants is to see his name just once in the obituary column.

He threatened to divorce her once, and she couldn't help shedding a few cheers.

She's leaving her money to charity and her brains to him.

When a neighbor told her she was getting a divorce from the meanest, crossest man in the world, she scoffed, "How can you get a divorce from my husband?"

She refuses to give him a divorce. She says, "I've suffered with the bum for fifteen years, and now I should make him happy?"

He brings home the bacon, but forgets the applesauce.

He forgets his wife's birthdays, but remembers her age.

When she married him, she exchanged the attentions of many men for the inattention of one.

He hasn't paid any attention to her in years, but he'll shoot any man who does.

The only time he shows her any real loving is when he takes her to a drive-in movie and lets her look in other cars.

Once he showed her some attention and it frightened the poor woman half to death.

Once a cyclone ripped their roof off and whirled them a half-mile through the air. It was the first time in years they were out together.

He's a perfect gentleman. When she drops something, he kicks it to where she can pick it up easier.

He's very thoughtful. He holds the door open for her when she staggers in with a load of groceries.

He's very considerate. He hasn't made his garden any bigger because she tires easily.

He's her greatest admirer. He places her on a pedestal—so she can reach the ceiling with her paint-roller.

She's sticking to him through thick and gin.

He has her do her reading in the closet so his sleep won't be disturbed.

As soon as she starts giving her side of an argument, he shuts off his hearing aid.

His timing is perfect—so is his two-timing.

He has circles under his eyes from keeping a triangle under his hat.

He doesn't mind his wife keeping her beauty secrets as long as he can keep his beauties.

Give him enough rope, and he'll be tied up at the office with his blond secretary.

He has found real happiness in marriage—his wife doesn't watch him too closely.

He gave his secretary a fur coat to keep her warm, and then had to give his wife one to keep her cool.

He thought he was pulling the wool over his wife's eyes, but he used the wrong yarn.

He's a homeless individual. Nobody is ever home less than he is.

His wife has two problems—him and the fire. Every time she turns to look at one, the other has gone out.

She married him in the belief that marriage is a union of two souls, but she finds herself hitched to a heel.

She spent the first part of her life looking for a husband; now she's spending the second part wondering where he is.

He's been in love with the same woman for fifteen years. If his wife finds out, she'll kill him.

He has a wife who appeals to his finer side, his loftier instincts, and his better nature—and a mistress who helps him forget them.

As a husband, he's the world's greatest lover—he has five mistresses.

If she ever catches him, the game won't be worth the scandal.

Hypochondriacs

He has an infinite capacity for faking pains.

He wants to have his ache and treat it too.

She always gives you a preamble to her constitution.

When he smells flowers, he looks around for a funeral.

If he finds a feather in his bed, he's sure he has chicken pox.

He always feels like a sick oyster at low tide.

He won't use ice cubes because he can't boil them.

She's always on pills and needles.

He won't kiss his wife unless her lipstick has penicillin in it.

She's always brooding over her health, but never hatches.

He takes so many different-colored sleeping pills, he dreams in Technicolor.

He has taken so many tranquilizers for the butterflies in his stomach, they're playing Ping-pong with them.

He's so afraid of surgery, he won't even read the *opening* pages of a book.

He always carries a thermometer behind his ear. He even stirs his drinks with it.

He's a stew going to pot.

She's taking drugs that haven't even been written up yet in *Reader's Digest*.

She not only complains of diseases for which there are no known cures, but of some for which there are not even known names.

He won't even talk on the phone to anyone who has a cold.

He's doctoring himself out of medical books. One of these days he's going to die of a misprint.

He's a manic-depressive type—easy glum, easy glow.

He's so full of penicillin, every time he sneezes he cures a dozen people.

She's unhappy because she has no troubles to speak of.

He's like a bus straphanger—he has complaints of long standing.

He'll never die in his sleep—he doesn't sleep that well.

He always feels bad when he feels good for fear he'll feel worse when he feels better.

She eats so much wheat germ to stay healthy that she sways in the breeze.

She calls a doctor when all she wants is an audience.

He collapses at the first twinge, pain, or ache like a dollar umbrella in a storm.

He's so impressionable that if he should come across the same name as his in an obituary column, he'd shoot himself.

She just can't leave being well enough alone.

He's leaving instructions in his will to be buried alongside of a physician.

She never takes a tranquilizer. She gets awfully agitated if she's not high-strung.

He's taken so many green and red pills, they're hiring him to direct the traffic.

She's a real woebegonia.

He has the same effect on you as a wet holiday.

He's as glum as a bankrupt undertaker.

You can never possibly know how she suffers—if you're way out in the woods somewhere, away from telephone, mail, or telegraph.

He can get into a stew faster than an oyster.

She spends most of her life at the complaint counter.

She has such a sour look that when she puts face cream on, it curdles.

His expression is as woebegone as a centipede's with bunions.

He has such a long face, his barber charges him twice as much for shaving him.

With that long puss, she'd be sure to win first prize in a cat show.

She's a misfortuneteller.

Idlers

He's a two-dimensional guy—he has loungitude and lassitude.

The only thing he grows in his garden is tired.

He heard that hard work never killed anybody, but he's taking no chances on being its first victim.

He's not afraid of hard work—he's fought it successfully for years.

He's stopped drinking coffee in the morning because it keeps him awake the rest of the day.

His wife is the power behind the drone.

Regularly every day he does his daily dozing.

He's too lazy to walk in his sleep—he hitchhikes.

He claims he's superstitious—he won't do any work in any week that has a Friday in it.

He puts off until tomorrow everything he has already put off until today.

He has a great laborsaving device—tomorrow.

Every morning he scans the obituary column; if his name isn't there, he goes back to bed.

He always looks forward to the yawn of new days.

He gets dizzy spells, which he attributes to his "prostrate" gland.

He complains of a bad case of insomnia—he keeps waking up every few days.

His wife has posted signs that read: "Hunters: Don't shoot anything in these parts that's not moving. It may be my husband."

The only difference between him and the Sphinx is that he moves when the dinner bell rings.

He's having a great life so long as he doesn't waken.

He's the idol of his family. He's been idle for five years.

His idea of roughing it is to turn his electric blanket down to medium.

He's rusting on his laurels.

He has a malady that malingers on.

Nothing is impossible to him—so long as he doesn't have to do it himself.

He needs two desks—one for each foot.

It would be interesting to know what his ambition in life is besides breathing.

He walks in his sleep so he can get his rest and his exercise at the same time.

His motto is: "Whatever is worth doing is worth asking somebody to do it."

He does most of his work sitting down—that's where he shines.

When he left his job, his fellow workers got together to give him a little momentum.

He discarded his How-to-Succeed books because they said you have to work for it.

With him, getting up in the morning is a conflict between mind and mattress.

The only things he fixes around the house are Martinis and Manhattans.

He doesn't like gardening because soil rhymes with toil.

He even hires a gardener to take care of his window-box plants.

If he lives long enough, he'll beat Rip van Winkle's record.

He bought a book, *How to Conquer Laziness,* and has his wife read it to him.

He smokes a clay pipe so that when it falls and breaks he doesn't have to stoop to pick it up.

He even gets winded playing chess.

He doesn't know how long he's been out of work—he can't find his birth certificate.

He's as active as a leftover fly in January.

He's as lively as a galvanized corpse.

There's as much life in him as in a mummy.

He's as torpid as a toad at the bottom of a well.

He's deader than a three-day-old bus transfer.

He's as indolent as an old bachelor.

He's as active as an oyster on the beach in August.

He has a very good background, and he's always leaning on it.

He wakes up in the morning with nothing to do, and goes to bed with it only half done.

Whenever he feels like exercising, he lies down on a couch until the desire passes.

He's always starting to begin to commence to get ready to do something.

He has become so lazy that even loafing is now hard work.

He has the seven-year itch, and he's three years behind in his scratching.

He's college-bred. He made a four-year loaf with his father's dough.

Asked by the census taker whether he was alive, his wife answered: "That's a matter of opinion."

His wife can't say how tall he is. It's been years since she's seen him standing up.

At the altar, he vowed their marriage would be for life. Now his wife wants to know why he doesn't show some.

He sleeps as soundly as a night nurse on duty.

He never puts off until tomorrow what he can put off indefinitely.

His greatest pleasure in life is having lots to do, and not doing it.

He claims he's a victim of mental anguish. Mental languish is more like it.

He does push-ups three times a day—from his big leather chair for meals.

Juvenile Delinquents

He carries a blackjack in his pencil box.

He's playing jacks—Jacks or better to open.

He's playing that nice old game of hopscotch. Only trouble is, he's playing it with real Scotch.

It's not bad enough that he's the toughest kid in the school, but he also has a perfect attendance record.

He's very careful about his health. He smokes only filter-tipped marijuanas.

He would rather steal hub-caps than third base.

His parents give him a free hand, but not in the proper place.

It takes more than understanding for his dad to be a pal to him—it takes stamina.

Instead of being coddled at school, he should be paddled by the Board of Education.

He's a real sadist. He locks the bathroom door on the nights of his grandfather's beer parties.

A good thrashing might get the wild oats out of him.

He's an honor student. He's always saying, "Yes, your Honor," "No, your Honor."

Everything in his home is controlled by switches—except him.

He was a lovable kid. They gave him a sandbox to play in. It should have been filled with quicksand.

He's too young to drive, so he's stealing chauffeured limousines.

He has just joined a union—a teenage mugger's union.

Today's accent may be on youth, but the stress is on the parents.

He has no respect for age unless it's bottled.

He belongs to a gang of boys who are alike in many disrespects.

He'd be smarter if he smarted in the right places.

Liars

He's a man of proven liar-bilities.

He's like a harp struck by lightning—a blasted lyre.

He's a confirmed liar—nothing he says is ever confirmed.

Some people take the bull by the horns—he shoots it.

He's a second-story man. No one ever believes his first story.

He's full of soft soap—mostly lye.

At college, he majored in alibiology.

He not only kisses and tells—he kisses and exaggerates.

He's such an exaggerator, he can't even tell the truth without lying.

A lie never passes his lips—he talks through his nose.

He needs a partition between his imagination and his facts.

He tells more lies than falsies.

He lies like an affidavit.

At a party he's the guy who always starts the bull rolling.

He couldn't even tell the truth in a diary.

You can't believe him, even when he swears he's lying.

He makes his bed and then tries to lie out of it.

He lies like a fellow with a secondhand car to sell.

His conversation is like a dice game—a lot of crap.

He lies on the sand in Miami Beach—about how important he is in his home town.

The only thing that keeps him from being a barefaced liar is his moustache.

He's like a microscope expert—he magnifies everything.

His lies aren't just white lies. As far as the truth is concerned, he's color-blind.

The trouble with his cooked-up excuses is that they're half-baked.

Marriage—
Present Tense

Marriage made the two one, but it's been a constant struggle to establish which one *is* that one.

She's a rag, a bone, and a hank of hair—and he's a brag, a groan, and a tank of air.

He got married because he was tired and she got married because she was curious. They're both disappointed.

They're well matched. He has a furtive look and she has a flirtive look.

It's a beef-stew marriage. She's always beefing and he's always stewed.

The only time they're stuck on each other is when they're plastered.

They make a good match—they're both always lit.

Television is a blessing for them. They would rather look at anything than at each other.

On Valentine's Day they follow their usual custom. They eat each other's heart out.

They're inseparable; it takes several people to pull them apart.

They have their little scraps, but nothing too serious. It doesn't need more than a couple of policemen to break them up.

No sooner did they say "I do" at their wedding than they started to look around to see if they could do better.

When he's in, she's out; when she's in, he's out. They can't find each other to discuss a divorce.

Marriage may be a 50-50 proposition. Unfortunately, they don't understand fractions.

They're petitioning the government to put all matters pertaining to marriage under the jurisdiction of the War Department.

Their unhappiness is due to illness—they're sick of each other.

They're a pair of lovebirds—always flying at each other.

They're incompatible. He has no income and she has no patibility.

They're very compatible. They both dislike each other.

They're as companionable as a cat and a goldfish.

They're as compatible as ham and matzos.

They're as unlike as a yacht and a coal barge.

They quarrel like two halves of a Seidlitz powder.

They get along like two peeves in a pod.

It started out as puppy love, and has since gone to the dogs.

You never hear an angry word from them—their apartment is soundproof.

They're proving that two can live as bitter as one.

Their home is frequently closed for altercations.

They've stopped dating and started intimidating.

They're always holding hands—if they let go they'd kill each other.

They're not just drifting apart—they're under full sail.

They used to keep a diary of their lovers' quarrels, but they had to give it up—it's become too big a scrapbook.

They'd be ashamed to sell their family parrot to the town gossip.

For years they've been racing for supremacy. It's high time they settled down to neck and neck.

They once swore to love—now they love to swear.

One marriage in four ends in a divorce—they're fighting it out to a finish.

If they had to do it over again, they'd still marry each other—at the point of a gun.

Marriage—
Past Tense

She's suing him for divorce because of reckless driving. He drove by her with a blonde.

He's being sued for divorce on account of a chronic ailment. He suffers from high blonde pressure.

She's getting a divorce on the ground of mental cruelty—like a couple of times he tried to kill her.

For years she's been suffering from a pain in the neck, so she's getting rid of him.

He's divorcing her because she has a sobering effect on him —she hides the bottle.

She's suing him for divorce and naming his mirror as corespondent.

She's asking for a divorce because he's more interested in spice than spouse.

She's divorcing him because he's just gotten out of a sickbed—his girl friend had the flu.

He was busy earning his salt, but she divorced him because he forgot the sugar.

She's suing for divorce because the man who was once her suitor no longer suits her.

She wants a divorce on the ground of desertion. She gave him enough rope, and he skipped.

He's asking for a divorce on the ground that he couldn't give her the world with a fence around it, so she gave him the gate.

He's suing for divorce on the ground that she threw his coat out. He happened to be in it at the time.

He wants a divorce on the ground that her upkeep is his downfall; he was fast on the deposit, but she was faster on the draw.

He divorced her because life with her was one canned, undarned thing after another.

His ground for divorce: for their anniversary she gave him a set of luggage—packed.

She's not divorcing him because there's any other man in her life. It's just that she's determined there will be.

They're in the divorce court because they regard their marriage tie as a forget-me knot.

They took the "for better or worse" vow, but they didn't say for how long.

They forgot that in "wedding" the *we* comes before the *I*.

It was love at first sight and ended at the first slight.

Their "I do" turned out to be much "I do" about nothing.

The trouble with their wedlock was that they misplaced the key.

The grave of their love was excavated with little digs.

Their divorce is hash made of domestic scraps.

The minister gave them a life sentence, but it was suspended in the divorce court for bad behavior.

Common sense might have avoided their divorce—and their marriage too.

She's on her way to Reno, the land of the free and the grave of the home.

Their married life was tense and their divorce the past tense.

Their marriage was a drama in three acts: Announced, Denounced, Renounced.

Their courtship was a quest, their marriage a conquest—the divorce was the inquest.

They're pressing their divorce suit with the seamy side out.

Their marriage was like a card game. It took two to open, and could have ended up with a full house if they hadn't thrown in their hands.

They're in the midst of a custody battle. She refuses to allow him to keep his mistress.

He got custody of the children and she got custody of the money.

She's a remarkable housekeeper. Every time she gets a divorce, she keeps the house.

It was a long-drawn-out divorce suit. His wife got half and her lawyer the rest.

She's been married three times and getting richer by decrees.

He had no idea when the judge granted the divorce that he had such a high cash-surrender value.

They're separated physically, but not financially.

They finally came to financial terms—hers.

As they left the divorce court, she whispered to him, "Bye now—pay later."

Ever since their divorce, he's getting the billing without the cooing.

The alimony payments are giving him a splitting headache.

She was unhappily married, but with her alimony she's happily unmarried.

Their marriage was a declaration of war, their divorce a declaration of peace, and the alimony is taxation without representation.

He married her in haste and is repenting insolvent.

Before the divorce, he complained of the high cost of loving. Now he's concerned with the high cost of leaving.

It was such a stiff alimony award in her favor, no wonder he calls it "alimoany."

Every time he has to meet an alimony payment, it's a case of wife or debt.

Although they're divorced, she still insists marriage has its compensations—alimony, for instance.

Meanies

If you kicked him in his heart, you'd break your toe.

He'll cry over your wounds so he can get salt in them.

He'd steal a dead fly from a blind spider.

He has as much use for anyone living as an undertaker.

He has a testimonial plaque from Simon Legree.

The only way he can hear any good about himself is to talk to himself.

He's applying for a job as a prison warden so he can put tacks in the electric chair.

He dreamed that he died and the heat woke him up.

His rough exterior covers a heart of flint.

He'd make dice out of his mother's knucklebones.

The only thing he'll share with you willingly is a communicable disease.

He heats the knives so his family won't use too much butter.

He shuts off his hearing aid when his wife offers her side of an argument.

He got his parents a fifty-piece dinner set for their golden anniversary—a box of toothpicks.

He's suffering from hardening of the hearteries.

He's taking up ventriloquism so he can go around throwing his voice under old maids' beds.

He's deaf and has never told his barber.

He sends get-well cards to hypochondriacs.

He told his children Santa Claus is too old to get around any more.

He'll give you the shirt off your back any time.

He takes sparrows, dips them in peroxide, and sells them as canaries.

He knifes you in the back and then has you arrested for carrying concealed weapons.

His wife wanted pearls for her birthday, so he gave her an oyster and a rabbit's foot.

He's buying a motel so he can rent cabins to old maids between honeymooning couples' cabins.

He'll throw a drowning man both ends of a rope.

He'd put his pet dog in a sputnik.

The last place he lived in, he campaigned for a dry law, got it passed—and then moved away.

Every time a scaring cigarette report comes out, he goes around blowing smoke in people's faces.

He's very sympathetic. He buries his head in his hands in the subway—he can't bear seeing an old lady standing.

He has a lot of fortitude—he'll stand for nearly anything but a woman on a train or a bus.

He hasn't stored up enough treasure in heaven to make the down payment on a harp.

He sheds tears, but they never reach his heart.

His motto is, "A tooth for a tooth"—but he expects yours to have gold in it.

He was engaged to a girl with a wooden leg. He got mad and broke it off.

He's so cold, he has to part his hair with an axe.

He's as hard-boiled as an Easter egg.

When his mother-in-law comes to visit, he buys her a jar of vanishing cream.

He's very friendly—he offers to take the postman out for a nice long walk on his day off.

He thinks everything is funny—so long as it happens to someone else.

He folds his newspaper so the guy next to him in the bus can read only half the headline.

On his employee's twenty-fifth year of loyal service he took back the watch he gave him fifteen years before, to have it overhauled.

He's a boss spelled backwards—double s.o.b.

His staff is quitting, not because of low wages, but because they're too tenderhearted to keep horses out of jobs.

As a boss, he believes hire should be lower.

He's so envious of others' possessions, he even sighed at his deceased friend's beautiful mausoleum, "That's living!"

He has a keen sense of humor—you can easily amuse him by slipping on an icy pavement, or on a banana peel.

The next time you'll meet anyone like him, it will have to be in a nightmare.

You couldn't warm up to him if you were cremated together.

Lots of people would enjoy working for him—if they were gravediggers.

Nudists

She grins and bares it.

He goes coatless and hatless with trousers to match.

She's never been accused of wrong undoing.

He sneaked his girl out of the nudist camp because he wanted to see what she looked like in a bathing suit.

From the time she joined the colony, every morning marked the dawn of a nude day.

She's wrapped up only in herself.

He joined the colony because he was anxious to see life in the raw.

He's the colony's Peeping Tom. He was caught looking through a knot hole at the girls passing by outside.

She's feuding with her boy friend—they're barely talking.

She's suffering from clothestrophobia.

He's the camp athlete. He runs 100 yards in nothing.

The police arrested her but they couldn't pin anything on her.

He was asked to grow a long beard so he could go to the village for supplies.

He was thrown out because he asked for dressing on his salad.

He was ostracized because his breath came in short pants.

She was expelled because she had a coat on her tongue.

When he drove into the camp for the first time, he even had to strip his gears.

Even her sewing machine is without a stitch.

They've asked her to leave. She demands panties on her lamb chops and jackets on her baked potatoes.

She broke off with her boy friend because they were seeing too much of each other.

You can't blame her for being the way she is—she was born that way.

Old Fogies

He's not the man he used to be—now his age is *really* showing.

His get-up-and-go has got-up-and-went.

That's not a gleam in his eye—it's just the sun hitting his bifocals.

There's spring in the air, but not in him.

All girls look alike to him.

Sunday night is the weak end of his weekend.

His thoughts have turned from passion to pension.

He's finding it tougher and tougher to make ends meet— such as his fingers and toes.

Now that he knows his way around, he doesn't feel like going.

He gets tired just wrestling with temptation.

His temper is getting shorter and his anecdotes longer.

He's buying moccasins so he won't have to lace his shoes.

When he has a choice of two temptations, he passes up the one that might keep him up late.

After a night on the town, he feels his oats—and his corns.

His daily dozen is followed by days of daily doesn't.

He has an off day after his day off.

He propositions a girl—and hopes she says No.

He's more interested in "yes" from his banker than from a blonde.

When he turns out the lights, it's for economy instead of romance.

It's getting so even making a long-distance call tires him out.

Lately, he keeps saying "I remember when" instead of "What's new?"

His plan for getting ahead is to stay even.

He's given up trying for home runs; he's satisfied just not to be struck out.

He complains, "I've run out of gas," and his wife believes him.

His wife powders and he puffs.

He not only has rheumatism—he has reminiscences.

He feels like a cigarette lighter. The spirit is willing but the flash is weak.

He's got gold in his teeth, silver in his hair, and lead in his pants.

The only thing he grows in his garden is tired.

The hardest things for him to raise in his garden are his knees.

He putters around the garden and mutters around the house.

It's taking him longer to rest than to get tired.

He's done long before the day is.

He's chock-full of pep—for an hour or two a day.

He considers a 10 P.M. TV program the Late Late Show.

He feels like the day after the night before, and he hasn't been anywhere.

His feet hurt even before he gets out of bed.

His forehead is getting higher and his energy lower.

He's begun to have thoughts about women instead of feelings.

His head is making dates that his body can't keep.

He hears one voice counseling "Why not?" and another, "Why bother?"

He pays more attention to the dish on the menu than to the dish who brings it in.

He's a WOW—A Worn-Out-Wolf.

He chases women only if it's downhill.

He picks up a woman's handkerchief, but doesn't pick up the woman.

Optimists

He puts his shoes on when a speaker says, "Now, in conclusion. . . ."

He asks his wife to help him with the dishes.

If he fell from the sixtieth floor of a skyscraper, he'd say, "So far, so good" at the thirtieth floor.

When he goes fishing, he takes along a camera and a frying pan.

On $60 a week take-home pay, he's marrying a girl who longs to have six children.

He saves the illustrations in seed catalogues to compare with the flowers and vegetables he grows.

He goes looking for an apartment with a drum in one hand and a saxophone in the other.

He's as bald as a billiard ball, but he buys hair restorers that have combs with every bottle.

He married his secretary, thinking he'd continue to dictate to her.

He blames the dry cleaner for his shrunken pants-waistband.

He starts working on a crossword puzzle with a fountain pen.

He starts figuring the taxes on $75,000 and $100,000 when trying to decide whether to buy one or two sweepstakes tickets.

All his life he's been a sinner, but he's taking harp lessons.

He goes into a hotel without baggage, and asks to have a check cashed.

He goes into a restaurant without any money, expecting to pay for the meal with the pearl he'll find in an oyster.

He looks for eggs in a cuckoo clock.

He's marrying at seventy, and is looking for a home near a school.

When he buys anything, he sees only the initial payment.

She sows wild oats and hopes for a crop failure.

She thinks her bulge is a curve.

Pessimists

He goes through life with morose-colored glasses.

Given the choice of two calamities, he chooses both.

She lives on the fret of the land.

He's a mountain climber over molehills.

He wouldn't be content with his lot even if it was a corner one.

He's constantly keeping his bad breaks relined.

Give him an inch, and he measures it.

She's always pulling tomorrow's cloud over today's sunshine.

He manages to find a little bad in the best of things.

To him, *O* is the last letter in "Zero" instead of the first letter in "Opportunity."

He has an optimistic stomach and a pessimistic digestion.

He's always building dungeons in the air.

He's always blowing out the light to see how dark it is.

Tell him that life begins at forty, and he laments, "So does rheumatism."

He's suffering from skeptic poisoning.

His usual greeting is: "Good morning, probably."

He never builds castles in the air for fear they'll have mortgages on them.

She broadcasts over such a fretwork of wrinkles, she needs to get her faith lifted.

He never worries about tomorrow—he knows everything is going to turn out wrong.

He wears not only a belt, but suspenders as well.

Wherever there's an optimist who sees a light where there is none, he's sure to be around to blow it out.

First things she looks for on entering a department store are the complaint and exchange counters.

He fills up every time he sees a gas station.

Playboys

So long as a woman has curves, he has angles.

He can take one look at a girl and tell what kind of a past she's going to have.

His love is just a passion fancy.

He studied meteorology so he could look in a woman's eyes and tell whether.

He loves his neighbors—especially their wives.

If a girl has the time, he has the place.

In his opinion, there's nothing like good music, good wine, a good meal, and a bad girl.

He starts with orchids and ends with forget-me-notes.

He treats all women as sequels.

He's the time of your wife at a party.

He has a terrific literary reputation; he's in practically every diary in town.

Women think at the start that he can be their soul mate, but he turns out to be a heel.

Nobody is his equal at making a peach cordial—he buys her a drink.

He believes a woman's best measurements are thirty-sex, twenty-sex, thirty-sex.

He's the kind of guy with whom a woman should eat, drink, and be wary.

When he gives a girl a string of pearls, he makes sure there's a string attached to it.

His motto is: "Life, Liberty and the Happiness of Pursuit."

All he knows about women is what he picks up—and, boy does he pick 'em up!

He's real broad-minded—in fact, he thinks of nothing else.

He's a man of single purpose and double talk.

You can always find him at a woman's door—the bedroom door.

He believes in nothing risqué, nothing gained.

He has a good line; first he talks about the weather, and then about the whether.

He gives a girl sloe gin to make her fast.

Give him an inch, and he takes the whole 36-27-35.

He encourages a woman to tell him about her past. Before she's through, he's part of it.

He always gives up something fancy for something fancier.

As a lover, he's a passing fiancé.

He has given up big game hunting for big dame hunting.

He's always on the lookout for the unbelievable—a passionate girl who is inconceivable.

His life is a bed of ruses.

The only footprints he'll leave on the sands of time will be the marks of a heel.

All he asks of a woman are two keys—to her heart and her apartment.

He's a wolf in chic clothing.

One thing is sure—he knows all the ankles.

At college, he signed up for all the romance languages.

Life for him is just one continuous round of dame foolishness.

He's the friendly type—always inviting women up to his apartment for a Scotch and sofa.

He has two hobbies—collecting old masters and young mistresses.

So far as he's concerned, love is just a passing fanny.

He loves babes—especially those born eighteen to twenty-five years ago.

He goes around with more women than a revolving door.

He specializes in women who believe in romance, while he depends on his eye-cue.

He treats women to rum and coax.

He's a reprobate who counts on a reduction in the wages of sin.

When it comes to seduction, he's always ready, villain, and able.

He gives women the kind of look that could be poured on waffles.

He can read a woman like a book, but he always forgets his place.

He's a modern dry cleaner. He works fast and leaves no ring.

Lots of women may not recall his name, but his hands are familiar.

He has wandering hands that go from pat to worse.

He's tall, dark, and hands.

He has submarine hands. Girls never know where they'll turn up next.

When he kisses a girl, he wishes their hearts would stand still—and she wishes she could say the same about his hands.

The way he dances, it looks like the vertical expression of a horizontal idea.

He's an expert on love—it's remarkable how he grasps the subject.

Everyone calls him "Chestnut" because he's nuts about chests.

He tells women he wants to be a good friend when all he wants is to be good and friendly.

He's a master of the art of getting attention without intention.

He got beaten up fighting for a woman's honor. Seems she wanted to keep it.

He was a victim one time of an air disaster—her husband flew home instead of returning by train.

When the wages of sin are paid, he'll get time and a half for overtime.

He thinks that sleep is the best thing in the world—next to a woman.

He just can't play straight with a girl who's all curves.

He believes if a good girl can't be led into temptation, then what is she good for?

He frequents resort hotels where when the bell rings at 6 A.M. everybody has to get out of bed—and return to his own room.

He only goes out with girls who wear glasses—he breathes on the lenses so they can't see what he's doing.

Even as an infant, he grabbed for the nurse instead of the bottle.

He only goes out with women who don't "no" too much.

He made a perfect 36 on the golf course, but she dropped him when she found out he was married.

He acts as if he had just invented sex and can't wait to spread the idea around.

When a woman resists his advances, he holds her for further questioning.

He likes dumb girls because a dumb girl is a dope, a dope is a drug, doctors give drugs to relieve pain—so a dumb girl is just what the doctor ordered.

He always hangs around a woman with a past in the hope that history will repeat itself.

As a guy who knows his oats, he sure can talk a girl into a serial.

If he ever went to Honolulu to see native dancers, he'd take a lawn mower along.

He likes to see a broad smile—when she's smiling at him.

He spends summers in the Alps, winters in Miami, and springs at blondes.

He prefers well-formed women to well-informed ones.

He always harps on the weather—whether she will or she won't.

He's a gentleman who befurs blondes.

Last New Year's he made a solemn resolution to cut down on wine and women. It was the most miserable afternoon he ever spent.

He's fast going to the dogs, chasing chickens.

He invites women to his farm and gets lofty ideas in the barn.

Every time he goes out with a woman, either she's married or he is.

His approach to love and romance is soft music, soft breezes, soft lights, and soft soap.

He's a yes-man with no interest in a no-girl.

His motto is: "Strike while the eyein' is hot."

He was in trouble recently for holding up a train. It was a bride's train and it seems he held it too high.

He's a regular Cashanova.

He'd be in clover if it wasn't for his wild oats.

When he gives a check to a girl, it's liable to bounce back, marked "Insufficient Fun."

They call him "Sailor"—he likes a little port in every girl.

He's waiting for the right girl to come alone.

He whistles while he lurks.

He's the kind that men don't trust too far and women don't trust too near.

No sooner is he alone with a sweater girl than he tries to pull the wool over her eyes.

When he hears that a woman has a past he goes to work to brighten up her present.

He not only knows how to hold a girl tight—he knows how to get her that way.

The only time he likes to see a girl stick to her knitting is when she's in a wet bathing suit.

He can count only up to sex.

Take a good look at him and his shoes and you'll see three heels.

THE PLAYBOY BOSS

He never hires a stenographer unless she's thoroughly sexperienced.

He pinches and scrapes at the office—pinches his secretary's cheeks and scrapes the lipstick off his own.

As a husband he acts like a boss, and as a boss he acts like a husband.

He demands of his secretary a period after every sentence—a recreation period.

He fired his secretary because of lack of experience. All she knew was shorthand and typing.

He's real ungrammatical—when dictating to his secretary he always ends a sentence with a proposition.

He's a perfect gentleman. All his secretary has to do is slap his face once in awhile.

His female employees aren't so tired of punching the clock as of punching him.

He's very pleased—she's the best little secretary he ever got his hands on.

He's an efficiency expert. He can juggle every figure in the office—including his secretary's.

He's a stockbroker, but he's busier trying to corner his secretary than he is the market.

He's an architect. He hired a curvaceous blond secretary—he has great plans for her.

He takes a look at his attractive secretary, and starts nightdreaming.

His stenographers have to have a lot of experience handling shorthand—and long arms.

He never passes up a chance to miss business with pleasure.

He dictates to his cigar, and gets his stenographer lit.

He doesn't play around during office hours—he likes them naughty but nights.

IN THEIR SECOND WOLFHOOD

He may be old, but he's still in there pinching.

He's an over-sexy over-sixty.

He's a little roué of sunshine.

He thinks he's a thing of beauty and a boy forever.

He's still chasing women, but he can't remember why.

He's in his second Brigitte Bardotage.

Taken to the hospital recently, he took a turn for the nurse.

All he asks of life is a little peach and quiet.

Some day he may realize that time wounds old heels.

He should be paying more attention to soaking his wild corns than to sowing wild oats.

At his age, all women look the same—good.

The old rapscallion hands out minks to keep some young blondes warm, proving there's no fuel like an old fool.

He's taking dancing lessons to teach his old dogs new tricks.

He believes he's still as good at attracting women as he never was.

He's an antiquated sugar daddy who takes a girl buy-buy—then she goes bye-bye with a younger guy.

He's a real cave man—one hug-and-kiss and he caves in.

He's keeping a young mistress. He knows at his age it may be fatal, but he says he doesn't know a better way to die.

This frisky, flirtatious eighty-year-old fossil's greatest ambition is to be shot by a jealous husband at ninety.

The girls all love this old "bird" for all he's worth—after he passes the assets test.

The romantic antique has a lot of trouble opening the

windows in his love nest. He now has them marked "His" and "Hernia."

The old reveler is going through that last-fling period when he isn't dangerous to anything except his reputation.

Playgirls

She has a Sunday-school face and Saturday-night ideas.

She's a capable girl—capable of anything.

She's a mere stripling—but how she can strip!

She may be a miss, but she doesn't miss much.

She's a girl that's game—everybody's.

The only time she says "Stop" is when she sends a telegram.

Her good times began when she had her no's fixed.

She's a lush blonde fast becoming a blond lush.

She looks like a little lamb, but she's really a wolf in she's clothing.

She's the proverbial good time that was had by all.

She knows the right answers, which is why she is often asked things out of the question.

Between her "No" and her "Yes" you couldn't stick a pin.

The best years of her life are figured in man hours.

She's like a flower—she grows wild in the woods.

171

She has a mink coat but she's still paying nightly installments on it.

There's a rumor she's pregnant—it's a miss-conception.

She's insulted when you offer her a drink, but she swallows the insult.

The only thing that can ever make her blush is the corner drugstore.

She never whispers sweet nothing-doings in fellows' ears.

She's been around more than a carousel.

She has a sunny disposition and a shady past.

She believes in affair play.

Offer her a Scotch and sofa and she's sure to recline.

It's a safe bet that she writes her diary in invisible ink.

She keeps her hair light and her past dark.

She has been tried and found wanton.

In the summer, you'll always find her at the beach in her baiting suit.

She's the demure, shy type—the kind you have to whistle at twice.

She knows how to say things with her torso that other girls waste a lot of time putting into words.

Her wink can give you a whether signal.

She's a cutie on the q.t.

She's preparing for a European tour—she's learning how to say "yes" in five languages.

She never hesitates when torn between vice and versa.

She has a sylphlike figure and doesn't keep it to her *sylph*.

Ask her if she's free for some night and she answers, "No, but I'll be reasonable."

She can give you a beau-by-beau account of her affairs.

She has a heart like the Army—open to all men between eighteen and forty-five.

She drinks sloe gin and is made fast.

She'd rather have beauty and curves than brains—she knows that the average man can see better than he can think.

Her theory is that girls who do right get left.

It's a lovely fur coat. She's not saying how much she played for it.

For a girl without principle, she draws considerable interest.

She's a public relations girl. Her biggest job is keeping her relations from becoming public.

She has a line that makes her popular—the line of least resistance.

She can't swim a stroke but she knows every dive in town.

Anyone can get her number—it's on the walls of phone booths all over town.

The way she flips her hips and tosses her torso, she has to be sin to be appreciated.

She's been on more laps than a napkin.

She can make five laps during a short party.

She's like a six-day bike rider—she finds it easy to make laps.

She says, "Who needs brains? Fellows don't whistle at a girl's brains."

When a fellow gets fresh, she counts to ten—thousand.

She claims she got her fur coat for a mere song, but more likely it was an overture.

She doesn't mind if her date is a cad, so long as his convertible is too.

She's leading a date-to-date existence.

She has hidden charms and she thinks it's silly to hide them.

She has shapely legs and she's proclaiming it from the hosetops.

Tight clothing is said to stop circulation, but so far as she's concerned, the tighter her clothing the more she's in circulation.

She's popular on account of her tight sweaters and loose habits.

She doesn't make a practice of necking. It's been years since she needed any practice.

She always obeys the boyological urge.

She won't go anywhere without her mother, and her mother will go anywhere.

She knows where bad little girls go—everywhere.

She's not a beauty—but is she a cutie!

She's an expert at keeping men hip-notized.

Marriage isn't important to her. She's willing to mate a man half way.

She has seen more of life in the raw than a night watchman in a nudist camp.

She moves in the best triangles.

There's an old saying, "You can never tell about a woman." In her case, it's charitable not to.

She doesn't know any four-letter words—like can't, won't, stop, and don't.

She's a *petite* girl—but she'd rather pet than eat.

She makes good impressions on the boys—with her lipstick.

She's the type who likes to be taken with a grain of assault.

Her father sells real estate and she gives lots away.

She lets her boy friend's conscience be her guile.

She advances pulses by not repulsing advances.

She knows that men make passes at girls who drain glasses.

She's like an automobile radiator—she'll freeze up on you if you don't fill her with alcohol.

The way she crawls away from temptation it invariably overtakes her.

She recently met a man in the strangest way—they were introduced.

She's the type who isn't picked out but picked up.

At seventeen, her voice started changing—from no to yes.

She'll scream at a mouse but will get into a convertible with a wolf.

The fellows think she's from the South, the way she says "You-all-may."

She goes with men who prefer women who know what men prefer.

She started out as a schoolteacher, but she never had any principal.

She's a postman's daughter and she's certainly fast with the males.

She's a parson's daughter and she sure has her following.

She's a shoemaker's daughter and she sure gives the boys her all.

She's a dressmaker's daughter and she's always making a slip.

She's a gardener's daughter and she knows all the rakes.

THOSE OFFICE CUTIES

Under "Experience" on the application blank, she wrote, "Oh, boy!"

She got the job when she wrote on the application blank: "No bad habits—willing to learn."

She failed the typing test but passed the physical.

She was hired on the basis of glamour—not grammar.

She can't add, but she certainly can distract.

She was three laps ahead of the nearest competition.

She's never been positionless because she's always inhibitionless.

She lost her last job because of illness—the boss's wife got sick of her.

Her salary goes up as her neckline goes down.

She's dangerous to have around the office—too many moving parts.

She's very efficient—never gets lipstick on the boss's collar.

She's very efficient—always manages to be out of the office when the boss's wife visits him.

She likes her job—lots of opportunities for advances.

She doesn't punch the time clock because she doesn't punch the boss.

She's the main squeeze in the office.

She looks for "bankruptcy" under the r's. She knows how to spell "bank"—she's looking for "ruptcy."

She has a remarkable brain. It starts working the moment she gets up in the morning, and doesn't stop—until she gets to the office.

She's the latest thing in secretaries—always an hour late.

She can't type so well, but she can erase 60 words a minute.

She has a great future. She's really going places—with the boss.

She's the perfect secretary—types fast and runs slow.

Her boss told her he'd pay her $85 a week with pleasure, but she said with pleasure she wanted $125.

She's a thoroughly sexperienced secretary.

She recently changed her position—the boss's wife made an unexpected appearance.

She makes an excellent deceptionist.

Her typing and spelling are improving—she may soon give up those tight sweaters.

The last two months of the year, she starts working her fingers to the bonus.

She always stops to think—trouble is, she forgets to start again.

When the little bell on her typewriter rings, she thinks it means a coffee break.

She's wearing low-cut dresses since the firm has been thinking of installing automation.

She says to her amorous lawyer-boss: "Stop, and/or I'll slap your face."

She shifts her typewriter into neutral and lets her tongue idle on.

She's tickled pink when she gets a job and she's tickled pink when she goes in for dictation.

She's been run around more desks in the office than a vacuum cleaner.

She's earning every cent of her salary. Her boss is so bowlegged, she's always falling through his lap.

She won't be around the office much longer because she's expecting too much—she's getting too big for her job.

Political Acrobats

He's full of promises that go in one year and out the other.

He stands for what he thinks people will fall for.

Honesty is his policy. When he's bought, he stays bought.

He has three hats: one to cover his head; one that he tosses in the ring; and the one he talks through.

He'll do anything for the worker but become one.

He approaches every question with an open mouth.

To him, politics is a game with two sides and a fence.

He always studies both sides of an issue so that he can get around it.

He never keeps his fences so high that he can't straddle them.

He's very acrobatic—he can straddle a fence while keeping his ear to the ground.

He has a straightforward way—of dodging issues.

He shakes your hand before election and your confidence after.

For him, the path of glory leads but to the gravy.

There's no doubt he's doing something about hidden taxes—he hides them better.

He's always trying to save both his faces.

He's sure to leave pussyfoot prints on the sands of time.

He refuses to answer any questions on the ground that it will eliminate him.

"Economy" is his slogan, provided it's not in his own district.

His political plums didn't grow from seed—they're the result of clever grafting.

His favorite menu is applesauce served with pork.

Around election time, he always announces his views, from his hedgequarters.

At the start of a campaign, he comes out shooting from the lip.

He fills the air with speeches, and vice versa.

He's standing on his record—to keep the voters from taking a good look at it.

He's skilled in the art of talking in circles while standing on "four-square."

No one can call him a cheap politician. Look how much he's costing the taxpayers.

He claims to be self-made, but he's really machine-made.

He's moving to an election district where the population is dense—from the neck up.

When he asks you to vote for him and for good government, he's asking you to vote twice.

He's running for office, but if they ever look up his record, he'll be running for the first plane to Rio de Janeiro.

He divides his time between running for office and running for cover.

He gets campaign contributions from the rich and votes from the poor on the pretense that he's protecting each from the other.

He finds out which way the crowd is going, then jumps in front and waves his banner.

He's mastered the art of appearing unenvious when he accuses his opponent of flimflamming the public.

His campaign slogan is: "I'm a simple man of the community." You can go still further and say he's the simplest man in the community.

You can count on him to lay down your life for his country.

He got himself elected by passing both the buck and the doe.

He's like the earth—he was flattened at the polls.

He tried to straddle an issue by staying in the middle, and he got hit from both sides of the fence.

Defeated at the polls, he can't decide whether he handed out too much baloney, or not enough.

His defeat is a real news story—a case of the bull throwing the politician.

Sad Sacks

If it rained soup, he'd have a fork instead of a spoon.

If he started out on a shoestring, everyone would start wearing loafers.

If he invested in an automobile stock, wagon trains would start making a comeback.

He's the kind of guy who falls on his back and breaks his nose.

He runs into accidents that started out to happen to someone else.

He married a girl for her money, and her dad went bankrupt the following week.

His ship finally came in, and sure enough there was a dock strike.

He has a wife and a cigarette lighter—neither one works.

He waited years for Dame Fortune to knock on his door, but it was her daughter, Miss Fortune, who showed up.

He bought a big house with lots of doors for Opportunity to knock on, but only his relatives did.

He's had the seven-year itch for eight years.

If he went into the men's pants business, men would start wearing kilts.

He started to fool with the market, but it was the market that did the fooling.

Just as his turn came for a check from the TV show "The Millionaire," the show went off the air.

He finally figured a way to make ends meet, but someone moved the ends.

He spent years developing skill as a second-story man, and along came ranch houses.

He worked two years on his boss's signature; then the perfectly forged check came back, marked "Insufficient Funds."

He's had bad luck with two wives. The first one left him and the second won't.

A couple of times he was crossed in love; then he got married and was double-crossed.

He picked a horse that he was sure would win in a walk, but the other horses ran.

He goes through life as handicapped as a cornet player with loose teeth.

His suit is so shiny, if it tears he'll have seven years' hard luck.

He went bankrupt three times and didn't make a cent once.

Just as a breeze blows a girl's dress up, it blows a cinder in his eye.

He has more ups and downs than a theatregoer in an aisle seat.

He wound up in jail for making big money—it was a quarter of an inch too big.

He's always in as tight a spot as a cork.

He's a yes-man, but he's working for a boss who always says No.

He worked a long time perfecting a bourbon toothpaste; when he had it just right, he no longer had any teeth.

He's a two-handicap golfer—he has a boss who won't let him off early and a wife who keeps him home weekends.

He was once shipwrecked on a desert island with his own wife.

He got a divorce and got custody of his wife's parents.

He was once a tree surgeon, but he kept falling out of his patients.

His bank account is his shrinking fund.

He made money as a men's pants manufacturer. Then he lost it on one skirt.

He followed the dictionary on buying stocks, where "invest" comes before "investigate."

He's had to give up his new home—it was on the outskirts of his income.

He's all set for a rainy day, with a pair of dry socks, rubbers, an umbrella, and a bottle of cold tablets.

Screwballs

His mother saw something in him that no one else saw—she saw that he was nuts.

He's getting a jacket for his birthday—the strait kind.

He's psychoceramic—a crackpot.

He has such a split personality, his psychiatrist had to buy a sectional couch for him.

He has such a split personality, his towels are marked "His" and "His."

He has such a split personality, his psychiatrist charges $50 each per visit.

I'm a-Freud he isn't all there.

Has he told you about his aberration?

He listens to his psychiatrist, and then draws his own confusions.

When he was born, no bells were rung—a pot was cracked.

He's as happy as if he were in his right mind.

185

His wife married him because she can't resist anything that's 50 per cent off.

They're thinking of putting him in the nut-house—for no reason at all.

His future position looks very secure—they're planning to put him in a strait jacket.

He reminds you of Whistler's mother standing up—he's off his rocker.

He has a one-crack mind.

In appreciation of his many years of service to the firm, they presented him with a gift certificate for two years' psychoanalysis.

He always eats in restaurants where they serve soup to nuts.

One look at him and you know why he's so self-conscious in the presence of monkeys.

He's as nutty as a fruit cake—as gone as a gone goose.

He carries a compass so he'll know whether he's coming or going.

His ideas are sure to be honeys—he has bees in his bonnet.

Maybe he's not nutty, but why does he stuff tobacco in his ears and ask for a light?

He's as sane as a lunatic's dream.

They call him "the Trainman"—he's plain loco and no motive.

They call him "Chocolate Bar"—he's half nuts.

The call him "the Liberty Bell"—he's half-cracked.

They call him "Bottletop"—he has a cork top and he's screwy.

He's stopped visiting his psychiatrist. He's an actor and he won't talk without a TelePrompTer.

Poor guy! He was in jail one time, and when they put him in charge of cooking the soup he went stir-crazy.

His psychiatrist is so expensive, all he gets for $25 is a get-well card.

His psychiatrist is so strict, he makes him stand up if he comes late.

He has an Irish psychiatrist—he uses a Murphy bed instead of a couch.

His psychiatrist asks him a lot of questions for a fat fee that his wife asks him for nothing.

He's learning how to stand on his feet while reclining on a couch.

He has a problem. If he doesn't pay his psychiatrists' bills, they'll let him go crazy, and if he pays their bills he'll certainly go crazy.

He goes to a psychiatrist who advertises this way: "Four couches—no waiting."

His psychiatrist has a new type of shock treatment—he sends his bills in advance.

Every year-end he gets a card from his psychiatrist reading, "Happy Neurosis!"

Sharpies

He always goes through a revolving door on someone else's push.

He's like French bread—not much dough, but lots of crust.

If he murdered his parents, he'd ask for mercy on the ground that he's an orphan.

He'd steal the teeth out of your mouth, and then come back for your gums.

He thinks he can substitute brass for brains.

He wouldn't hesitate to drive up to the gate of heaven and honk.

He picks up a girl on another fellow's whistle.

He'd ask for a coffee break if he worked for a tea company.

He picks up your chick instead of the check.

With his gall, he can hand back a letter for a third retyping to a steno he's playing around with.

As an executive, he delegates all the authority, shifts all the blame, and takes all the credit.

He got a bill with a notation on it: "This bill is one year old." He returned it with his own notation: "Happy birthday!"

He has nerve enough to flirt with a woman standing in a bus while he's sitting.

He's brazen enough to take a taxi to bankruptcy court and then ask the driver in as another creditor.

He sold two milking machines to a farmer with one cow, and then took the cow as a down payment.

He's always nice to waitresses—he plays them for big steaks.

He's a sly fox. He always manages to get what a wolf is after.

He can convince his wife she looks fat in a fur coat.

He can tell you to go to hell so persuasively, you actually look forward to the trip.

A woman tried to talk him into buying her a dress, and he talked her out of the one she was wearing.

He bought his wife some fine china so she wouldn't trust him to wash the dishes.

He can change a subject faster than a dictionary.

He sells cigar butts to midgets as king-sized Havanas.

He pins badges on frankfurters and sells them as police dogs.

He was a bellboy once in a swank hotel. Called for a deck of cards, he came up fifty-two times.

He keeps his wife on a pedestal so she can't put her foot down.

He's as cautious as two porcupines making love.

The last two months of the year he starts working his fingers to the bonus.

He hasn't let a woman pin anything on him since he was a baby.

He's looking for a rich girl who's too proud to have her husband work.

He's a man with coffee nerves. He has the nerve to take more than two coffee breaks.

Show-oafs

He thinks he's the life of the party. Actually, he's the laugh of the party—and the laugh's all on him.

He has one of those fun-track minds.

His idea of fun is throwing an egg into an electric fan.

At a party, he's the guy that always starts the bull rolling.

He makes you wonder why all the clowns you see around aren't in the circus.

He should have his jocular vein cut.

He's a comedian of the first water—a big drip.

He has a brother in prison who is also very popular—the lifer of the party.

The only place he has hair is on his jest.

He's a real vocalamity.

He sure has a good line. Too bad he doesn't hang himself with it.

He's snappy on the comebacks—like his checks.

Everyone takes his remarks with a grain of epsom salts.

He'll ask a question, answer it himself, and then tell you what's wrong with it.

He's the kind of show-off who's showed up in a showdown.

He blows his horn the loudest, but that's because he's in the biggest fog.

He thinks he knows it all, and keeps proving he doesn't.

He always manages to open something by mistake—his mouth.

As a cut-up, he missed his vocation. He should have been a barber.

Everyone calls him "Paul Revere" because he's always horsing around.

He's the life of the party, until it comes to picking up the check.

He looks like an owl and behaves like a jackass.

He's a real party live-wire—not only on his toes but on everyone else's.

His wife always begs him, "Now, if it's a dull party, just leave it that way."

He thinks he's a gay young buck—he isn't even two bits.

He's as popular as a mouse at a women's club meeting.

He needs only two glasses to make a spectacle of himself.

He thinks he's amusing, but he couldn't even entertain a doubt.

He's been nicknamed the "Surgeon"—he's a real cut-up.

She's the belle of every party—everyone wants to wring her neck.

He has a repertoire of three jokes all told—and told and told.

He thinks he electrifies a party, but he merely gasses it.

He's as loud as a Christmas tie and just about as welcome.

He graduated from college *magna cum loudest*.

He's the kind of braggart with whom it is no sooner done than said.

She's a real clamor girl.

He's always offering "sound advice"—99 per cent sound and 1 per cent advice.

He could never be a janitor. He's always putting out an over-supply of hot air.

If you took the air out of that big wheel, all that would be left of him would be a flat tire.

He has a voice like a buzz saw striking a rusty nail.

She thinks she's a siren, but she only sounds like one.

She's always mistaking the right of free speech for free screech.

Every time he opens his mouth he puts his feats in.

He's such a show-off, he even boasts that he's losing his mind.

She has a gum-chewer's mouth—it goes without saying.

At every party he's the M.C.—Mental Case.

They call him "Asthma"—he's so full of old wheezes.

At a party, he's loudmouthed, egotistical, and obnoxious,

but in spite of all that, there's something about him that repels everyone.

Someone once told him to be himself. He couldn't have been given worse advice.

Snobs

She should go to a plastic surgeon to have her nose lowered.

He claims he dines with the upper set—he uses his lowers too.

They hired an upstairs maid—and they live in a ranch house.

He's one of the Bore Hundred.

They've just bought a statusfying home.

They're only flakes off the upper crust.

He's such a blue blood, he never uses a fountain pen when he writes. He just cuts his finger.

The way she acts, you'd think it was her duty to be snooty.

Their old butler is serving their third degeneration.

She's one of those women who snoop and snub.

They belong to the upper crust—a lot of crumbs sticking together.

He looks like something that's been stuffed by a good taxidermist.

She's as stuck-up as a billboard.

He's proof that an empty head and a stuffed shirt can go together.

He's trying to go from the cash register to the social register.

They belong to the kind of country club where the men are stuffed shirts and the women are stuffed shorts.

She was born with her face lifted.

She has so many jewels, she's getting too big for her brooches.

She returns from her tours brag and baggage.

They're always talking about their inferiors, but no one has ever been able to find them.

She has the kind of look that hangs a price tag on every object in the room.

She struts around as if she were balancing her family tree on her nose.

He's so ritzy, he wears a riding habit just to pitch horseshoes.

She's so fashionable, if she decided to shoot her husband, she'd wear a hunting oufit.

Her head is so uplifted, she has a double chin on the back of her neck.

She even wallpapers the insides of the medicine chest and the refrigerator.

He claims he dines with the brass—which is quite understandable. They wouldn't trust him with the silver.

He may be listed in *Who's Who*, but he doesn't know what's what.

She belongs to the uppish classes.

He's as snooty as a clerk in a swank shop ringing up "No Sale" on a $25 purchase.

Her nose is so upturned, everytime she sneezes she blows her hat off.

She's as overbearing as a woman giving birth to quadruplets.

What a snob!—he must be inclined as the prig was bent.

The only thing he ever did for a living was inherit.

He'd feel snubbed if an epidemic overlooked him.

He claims his ancestors came over on the Mayflower— the immigration laws are much stricter now.

He paid a big fee to have his genealogy looked up, and now he's paying a bigger one to have it hushed up.

His family tree was started by grafting.

His family tree could stand a lot of trimming.

He boasts about his family tree—he comes from the shady side.

He claims his ancestors spring from a long line of peers— three of them sprang off the docks.

The best part of his family tree is underground.

He should be less concerned with what he's descended from and more concerned with what he's descended to.

He wants to be one of the Four Hundred; the way he's getting his money to achieve it, he's liable to wind up as Number 400.

She's studying geometry to learn how to move in the best circles.

They had their baby kidnapped so they could get their pictures in the papers.

They have wall-to-wall carpeting, wall-to-wall windows and back-to-the-wall financing.

They're going into debt trying to keep up with people who already are in debt.

They have an exquisite Morris chair in their living room, but Morris is taking it back.

They buy lovely period furniture—it's only a short period before the installment people take it back.

They claim they belong to the early settlers but you'd hardly think so judging by the bill collectors on their front steps.

They have holes in their sleeves trying to rub shoulders with the society crowd.

Even when they're finally buried underground, they'll try to keep up with the mausoleum crowd.

Their idea of social prominence is to have their names found everywhere—except in the phone book.

They forget that God created the world in a round shape so that no one could be first in a circle.

They're getting an awful inferiority complex—they've just met someone as good as they are.

Speakers

He gives you in length what he lacks in depth.

He's a dry talker who is usually all wet.

He covers indefinite ideas with infinite words.

His speeches are like the horns of a steer—a point here, a point there and a lot of bull in between.

When he finally finishes his speech, there is a great awakening.

His speeches go over like a pregnant woman trying to pole-vault.

He can usually rise to an occasion, but he doesn't know when to sit down.

He appeals to the emotions by beating the eardrums.

He's a sound speaker—oh, those sounds!

Only one man applauded; he was slapping his head to keep awake.

He speaks straight from the shoulder. Too bad his remarks don't start from higher up.

He claims to be speaking for posterity; if he isn't quick about it, they'll be along to hear it.

He doesn't put enough fire into his speeches. It would be better if he put his speeches into the fire.

All he needs to get his second wind is to say, "And now, in conclusion. . . ."

As a speaker, he's like a ship. He toots loudest when in a fog.

He gave a moving speech—long before he finished his audience had moved out into the hall.

He uses a lot of verbiage to say little about nothing.

His audiences never drink coffee before his after-dinner speeches—it might keep them awake.

He can dive deeper into a topic than anyone else, remain down longer, and come up drier.

He needs no introduction—what he needs is a conclusion.

He can make you feel numb on one end and dumb on the other.

His speech is like a bad tooth—the longer it takes to draw it out, the more it pains.

His audiences not only keep looking at their watches, they shake them.

The fault with many speakers is that you can't hear what they're saying. The trouble with him is that you can.

He hasn't a watch with him to time his talks. He should look at the calendar on the wall behind him.

Listening to his speeches, you can't help wondering who writes his immaterial.

He doesn't strike oil even in an hour, but he keeps boring.

His speech is like a wheel—the longer the spoke, the greater the tire.

His chairmen never say, "Our speaker needs no introduction." He needs all the introduction he can get.

Toastmasters can introduce him, but they can't guarantee him.

If all the people who have to sit through his speeches were lined up three feet apart, they would stretch.

He has his tongue in your ear and his faith in your patience.

In biblical days, it was considered a miracle when an ass spoke. Listening to him, you can't help but realize how times have changed.

Arrangement committees never see the need to supply him with a filled pitcher—you can't run windmills with water.

He never learned to leave his audience before his audience leaves him.

His speeches should be like a woman's skirt—just long enough to cover the subject, and short enough to create interest.

Tactless Boors

He has the manners of a gentleman. Obviously, they don't belong to him.

He's a rarely well-mannered person—very rarely.

We've all heard soup gargled and siphoned, but he yodels it.

The way he drank his soup in a nightclub, ten couples got up and danced.

He eats with his fingers and talks with his fork.

He has a nose that is not only seen but heard.

He's as refined as a cabbage.

He's as at home in refined company as a pig in a parlor.

The greatest points of interest in his life are 7 and 11.

He's such a lowbrow that when he gets a headache, he puts the aspirin in his shoe.

The only way he can live up to his ideal of himself is from a hole in the ground.

When he drops cigar ashes on a host's rug, he spills his Scotch and soda on it to prevent a fire.

As a tourist, his slogan is: "Stop, Look, and Litter."

He's a contact man—all con and no tact.

He would walk into an antique shop and ask, "What's new?"

He's tactless enough to tell a woman that something is as plain as her face.

The only high thing he's ever concerned with is the cost of living.

He's completely bald, but that still doesn't make him a highbrow or a polished individual.

He can talk louder than a TV commercial.

He's a real gentleman—he'll never strike a woman with his hat on.

He's lower than a horse's hoof or a baboon's forehead.

He's disappeared from his usual hangouts and hasn't been obscene since.

He thinks he's refined because he knows which fingers to put in his mouth when he whistles for the waiter.

He has dirty fingernails, and a mind to match.

He's never troubled by improper thoughts—in fact, he enjoys them.

He has one of those mighty minds—mighty dirty.

He's a fast eater. He starts on his dessert before the echo of his soup has died away.

He has an approach like a dentist's drill.

He smokes the kind of cigars that hold you smellbound.

He is very class-conscious. He has no class and everyone is conscious of it.

He has a laugh like the screech of a rusty door.

He dances like a cattle stampede.

He's as shallow as a pie pan.

He has a one-track mind—a dirt track.

The only way he's ever tidy is when he drinks his whiskey neat.

His neighbors call his TV set the "Astronaut" because it has conquered the air.

He's a fellow of a few, ill-chosen words.

His hair must be loaded with electricity with all those shocking things on his mind.

The only uplifted thing about her is her bust.

Her escort wouldn't mind her eating so much when he takes her nightclubbing, if he could only hear the orchestra.

She has foot-in-the-mouth disease.

The only person he's ever treated with kid gloves is a finger-print expert.

Tightwads

He thinks the world owes him a giving.

He got his money the hoard way.

He drinks with impunity—in fact, with anyone who'll buy.

The only time he picks up a check is when it's made out to him.

He's so tight, when he winks his kneecaps move.

He has low pockets and short arms.

When it comes to picking up a dinner check, he has an awful impediment in his reach.

He does his Christmas shopping surly.

Someday a check is going to reach out and grab him.

He gave his wife a ring that once belonged to a millionaire—Woolworth.

He wouldn't even buy happiness if he had to pay a luxury tax on it.

It's an art the way he avoids picking up a check. You have to hand it to him.

You can get anything from him for the asking—and, boy! the eyes, arms, and legs he's asking.

He takes his wife window-wishing regularly every week.

He's such a bargain-hunter, he married a half-wit because she was 50 per cent off.

When he goes on a week's vacation, all he spends is seven days.

He has never taken up hunting because he can't find a store that sells used bullets.

He believes charity begins at home—and should stay there.

He's a lady-killer—when he takes out a girl he starves her to death.

He talks through his nose to save wear and tear on his teeth.

He's the first to put his hand in his pocket—and keep it there.

He's so cheap he never takes anything but a sponge bath.

When his old mother visits him, he takes possession of her false teeth so she won't eat between meals.

He hasn't ever cut much ice because he's a real cheapskate.

His motto is: "Money doesn't grow on sprees."

He always has his nose in a book. He's too stingy to use a handkerchief.

He insists two drinks are enough for anyone—especially if he's paying for the third.

After the doctor gives him a blood test, he demands his blood sample back.

He got his parents a fifty-piece dinner set for their golden anniversary—a box of fifty toothpicks.

He's so small, if he ever sat on a dollar, ninety-five cents would show.

He tosses quarter tips around like manhole covers.

He's so stingy, he won't even tip his hat.

He orders asparagus and leaves the waiter the tips.

When he says it's not the money but the principle of the thing, you can be sure it's the money.

He's heard that you can't take it with you, but he says if he can't take it with him he won't go.

The way he nurses a Scotch and soda you'd think it was an hourglass.

He's an I.W.W. filling station customer. He stops only for Information, Wind, and Water.

If he drank poison, he'd try to get the deposit back on the bottle before passing away.

You know it's really summer when he throws out his Christmas tree.

He never paws a girl. His hands are too busy hanging on to his wallet.

He takes a girl to a drive-in restaurant, and then won't open the window.

He's always living within his relatives' means.

He has a greater love for specie than the species.

The only thing he ever gave away was a secret.

When it comes to doing some good he gives the Lord credit. Too bad he doesn't give some cash too.

He clasps his hands so tight in church during prayers that he can't get them open when the collection box comes around.

He takes a keen interest in the sermon, but only a passing interest in the collection.

He throws money around like a man without arms.

He goes out with his girl Dutch treat—they dance check to check.

When the brakes of his car give way, he tries to hit something cheap.

The way he reaches for a check, he must have inspired the inventor of slow-motion movies.

He'd skin a flea for its hide and tallow.

He's so grudging, when everyone else gives three cheers he gives two.

He'll sit through three showings of a lousy movie to get his money's worth.

Money flows from him like drops of blood.

He'd give you the sleeve out of his vest.

He tears the December page off the calendar during the Christmas season to fool his children.

He's so closefisted, he only gives you one finger when he shakes hands.

When he pays you a compliment, he asks for a receipt.

His pockets always outlast the rest of his suit.

He's so niggardly, he takes his kids' glasses off when they're not looking at anything.

He's always trying to get something for nothing, and then complains about the quality of the service.

If he ever found a box of corn plasters, he'd start wearing tight shoes.

He's so stingy, when he lets out a breath of air, it's practically a vacuum.

He's the kind of guy who drinks on an empty pocket.

He's a cheerful giver—cheerful because he gets away with giving as little as possible.

His wife expected roses on their anniversary, so he came home with Four Roses—on his breath.

He had a brass band at his wedding—he put it on his bride's finger.

He's taking up singing lessons because the scale begins and ends with "do."

He won't buy rattles for his kids. He lets them grab his nose and he shakes his head.

Anyone can borrow his lawn mower. It has a coin slot on it.

He can drink for hours—but that's before he gets to his own booze.

He's so tight, he even refuses to perspire freely.

He puts boric acid on his grapefruit in order to get a free eyewash.

Money is the last thing he thinks of—just before going to bed.

He's suffering from costrophobia—the fear of parting with a buck.

He's so close, he won't even let you borrow trouble.

He's a nodding acquaintance. Ask him for a loan and he says, "Nodding doing."

He keeps ten-dollar bills folded so long, Hamilton gets ingrown whiskers.

On their 40th wedding anniversary, he sent his parents forty pieces of silver—forty dimes.

He figured out a good way to save money on his honeymoon—he went on it alone.

Before spending a buck, he considers carefully how it will affect his favorite hobby—hoarding money.

His standard apology for not lending a friend any money is that it's all tied up in currency.

He drinks a glass of soda—then he tickles a mule to get a kick out of it.

He went to a swank seashore resort and got a suntan. When he got the bill, he turned white again.

His friends have an apt nickname for him—"the Doughnut."

He'll lend you an umbrella, and then takes it back when it starts to rain.

You can easily spot him in a nightclub. He's the one who's sitting with his back to the check.

His tailor has a problem—how to make a suit for him with one-way pockets.

He uses the same calendar year after year.

You can always find him where his best friend is—his bankroll.

He wouldn't ever get into a fight—not unless it was a free-for-all.

He's still single. Every time he was ready to get married, the price of rice went up.

He pays as he goes, except when he goes with somebody—and he always goes with somebody.

He's satisfied to let the rest of the world go buy.

Un-Altar-able Beaus

When a girl asks him for a diamond ring, he turns stone-deaf.

Women are always trying to drive him to the altar, but they can't make him link.

He adores women, but he doesn't let the feeling become nuptial.

He wants only one single thing in life—himself.

His wallet is full of pictures of near Mrs.

He avoids bride-eyed women.

In the land of the free and the home of the brave, he would rather be free than brave.

He avoids entanglements with women who would rather knot.

He never takes yes for an answer.

When he speaks of "tying one on," he doesn't mean an apron.

He believes in the guarantee of life, liberty, and the happiness of pursuit.

He's a fellow of un-altar-able views.

No one is more miss-informed than he is; he can only be miss-led so far.

He does right and fears no man; he doesn't write and fears no woman.

He has no children—to speak of.

He's a gay dog and no woman has ever been able to get him spousebroken.

His life is a bed of ruses.

One time he was crazy to get married, but he says that fortunately he realized it in time.

He's skilled at one-handed driving without skidding into a church.

He has been seen everywhere with a woman—except at the altar.

When he chases a woman, he makes sure not to catch her.

He hasn't got a thing against marriage—and he wants to keep it that way.

He sees no point in buying a cow when milk is so cheap.

He has yet to meet a woman whom he couldn't live with-out.

His motto is: "What God has put asunder, let no man join together."

The minute a girl starts asking her mother for recipes, he does a fast fade-out.

Just because he falls in love with a dimple, he sees no reason to marry the whole girl.

There's one gift he never gives a girlfriend—an electric blanket with dual controls.

His married men friends may have better halves, but he prefers his better quarters.

The only woman who ever pinned anything on him was his mother, when he was a baby.

He has a leaning toward women, but he never falls.

He always looks before he lips.

He believes in wine, women, and so-long.

All his romances have been carried off without a hitch.

He's always foot-loose and fiancée free.

His only objection to love is that it can become parsonified.

In his estimation, even once in a wifetime is too much.

He believes that being marriage-minded is a mental condition—when the mind is out of condition.

The only months in which he'd consider getting married are those that have a "w" in them.

To him, marriage is just a lot of dame foolishness.

Every morning he arrives at his office from a different direction.

He's a man of double purpose but single thought.

Wives

(THE BALL AND CHAIN)

She's sticking to him through all the trouble he never would have had if he hadn't married her in the first place.

He remembers when and where he got married, but what escapes him is *why*.

He takes his daytime problems to bed with him—she's opposed to separate bedrooms.

When he first married her, he could have eaten her alive. Now he's sorry he didn't.

He believed in dreams—until he married her.

He calls her the salt of the earth—he's been trying to shake her for years.

Asked how long he's been married, he says forlornly, "Every minute of the day and night."

He's just been given two months to live—that's how long she'll be away on vacation.

He blames his troubles on Adam for not having been adamant.

What he likes about her is that she drives him out to seek his happiness elsewhere.

A jeweler urges him to smother her with diamonds, but he's got a cheaper way in mind.

A friend told him, "My wife is an angel." "You're lucky," he commented, "Mine's still living."

She's so suspicious, if she finds no blond, black, or red hairs on his jacket, she accuses him of running around with bald women.

He should have know how jealous she is—she had male bridesmaids.

She left him once; then she came back again—she couldn't bear his having such a good time.

She swore she wouldn't talk to him for a month and he's unhappy about it—the month is almost up.

She has no minor voices.

This is his second marriage. He's been unlucky in both—his first wife left him and this one won't.

He insists Early American customs haven't changed—the Indian is not the only one who sleeps with a battle-axe by his side.

He shot a guy who planned to run off with her—the fellow changed his mind.

When he first announced that he had half a mind to marry her, he didn't realize that's all it required.

He never knew what happiness was until he married her—now it's too late.

He's the third man she's led to the halter.

Her towels are labeled His, Hers, and Next.

He should have been warned when he read the inscription on her last husband's tombstone: *"Rest in Peace—Until We Meet Again."*

He's bequeathing everything to her, provided she remarries within six months after his death. He wants someone to feel sorry he died.

He's leaving her because of another woman—his mother-in-law.

He's trying real hard to drown his troubles, but he can't get his wife and mother-in-law near the water.

He offers to send her mother to Africa at his expense to teach the Mau-Maus how to fight dirty.

He's a big success, and in back of him stand his wife and her mother—telling him how stupid he is.

BABBLERS

He has given her the best ears of his life.

She's an angel—always up in the air and harping on something.

The only chance he has of getting her to listen to him is to talk in his sleep.

He had laryngitis for three weeks, and didn't know it.

They're always having words, but they're always hers.

Every time he argues with her, words flail him.

He speaks six languages, she speaks two—just the right handicap.

They both wear pants, but it's not difficult to tell them apart —he's the one that's listening.

He can read her like a book, but he can't shut her up like one.

He's overweight. He became that way because eating gave him a chance to open his mouth.

She's wrecking the matrimonial bark with her matrimonial barking.

He carries pictures of the children—and a sound track of her.

He should have picked her with his ears instead of his eyes.

She's easily entertained—all he has to do is listen to her.

He has two mouths to heed—hers and her mother's.

Their marriage is a partnership—he's the silent partner.

He spends a good deal of his time by a babbling brook, because he can't brook her babbling.

When they first met, she looked like a siren. Now she talks like one.

He's happy when she's in bed, safe and soundless.

He has several mouths to feed, and one big one to listen to.

She hasn't spoken to him for a week. He's wondering what to give her to show his appreciation.

She's so tired at the end of the day, she can hardly keep her mouth open.

Their marriage is the walkie-talkie type. She's all talkie, which makes him go for a walkie.

If he wants to get in a word with her, he has to sit sidewise.

He's a good listener. He can't break in because she won't break off.

She not only has the last word when he argues with her—she has the last two thousand.

He went to a New Year's Eve party without noisemakers—but he had her along.

She believes in free speech. She's certainly free enough with hers.

They have words, but he never gets to use his.

He got rid of the noise in the back of the car—he made her sit up front.

He's in favor of safety-belts. She's a back-seat driver, and he'd love to give her a belt.

He doesn't know what she thinks of his new dentures—he never gets a chance to open his mouth.

She's already had four dentures. She wears them out with her tongue.

He calls her "Echo" because she always has the last word.

He wishes he had married a stutterer so he could get a word in now and then.

She had laryngitis once and it was like having the phone discontinued.

She chatters so much on the phone, he's asked the telephone company to come and remove her.

Talkative?—she was married to her first husband five years before she discovered he was deaf and dumb.

He has just drawn his last will and testament. The first line reads: "At last I have a chance to open my mouth."

HOUSEKEEPERS

When she put her finger through the wedding ring, it was the last thing she did by hand.

She thinks her work was done when she swept down the aisle.

She's not bothered when her husband reads the papers at breakfast—she never gets up for breakfast.

Before they were married, she promised she'd keep her kitchen immaculate. She's kept her promise—they eat out.

She'll put on almost anything for dinner, except an apron.

The only exercise she gets is running up bills and jumping to conclusions.

She's dissatisfied with their house because the household appliances aren't automatic—she has to turn on a switch.

The only reason her hair looks like a mop is that she doesn't know what a mop looks like.

She's one of those modern wives who believes in love, honor, and disarray.

Her closet would be messy even if she lived in a nudist camp.

As a housekeeper, she sweeps the room with a glance.

Her husband is very persevering. He can get to the bottom of most anything, except her pocketbook.

The only time she looks just right to him is on Halloween.

Her house is such a mess, when the phone rings she can't find it.

They're celebrating their tin wedding anniversary—five years of eating out of tin cans.

She can dish it out, but she can't cook it.

It takes her an hour to cook Minute rice.

She dresses to kill, and cooks the same way.

He brings home the bacon and she burns it.

They don't have pot roast—they have roast pot.

She must be very religious and a very loving wife. Every night at dinner time she places burnt offerings before him.

When their apartment burned down, it was the first time the food was hot there.

He takes one look at her burnt offering and exclaims, "What in cremation is it?"

He can always tell when they're having salad for dinner—he doesn't smell anything burning.

Life for him is one canned thing after another.

First thing he asks when he gets home at night is, "What's thawing?"

You never thaw such meals as she serves.

She was amazed when a neighbor told her you don't open an egg with a can-opener.

Her husband is a real gentleman. He never tells the true reason why the family prays before each meal.

She's kept her schoolgirl complexion, but you can't say that she's done much for his schoolboy digestion.

HIS GETTER-HALF

They're a balanced couple. He makes the money and she spends it.

She couldn't stand his ways, but she married him for his means.

She cares not one bit for him, but she lives on his account.

He thought she was going to make him a home, but she just made him.

She vowed at the wedding "to love and to cherish until debt do us part."

He's handsome. When she wants money, he has to hand some.

All the period things she buys are keeping him baroque.

He married her 125 checkbooks ago.

She made him a millionaire. Before she married him he was a multi-millionaire.

She gets expensive rocks from him, but she's otherwise stone-deaf.

He thinks nothing is too good for her—and so does she.

She's very gifted—he has the bills to prove it.

She's a human dynamo—she charges everything.

She can bring more bills into the house than a congressman.

Her upkeep will be his downfall.

She married him because he looked like a good support.

She cries a lot—not so much to get things out of *her* system as out of *his*.

She can get a mink coat out of him without half crying.

Her clothes make her, and break him.

He'll soon be destitute because she's dresstitute.

She has positively, absolutely nothing to wear—and four closets to keep it in.

She's sticking to him because he has a will of his own—and it's made out in her favor.

They were having their pictures taken, and the photographer told her to look natural—so she posed with her hand in his pocket.

She had only four requirements for a dutiful, loving husband—cash, stocks, bonds, and real estate.

The way she can spend money, he should become a counterfeiter.

Watching her purchases, he's constantly amazed to see all the things she'd rather have than money.

He's giving her the best expense-account years of his life.

When she goes shopping, she comes back with everything but money.

She can't cook or clean, but she can lick her weight in trading stamps.

The food she serves is not only high in calories but high in trading stamps.

She's less interested in her cookbook than in his checkbook.

They have a joint checking account. He puts in the money and she draws it out.

When he reproaches her for buying things as if there was no tomorrow, she says, "Name me one other extravagance."

She's a woman who's five years ahead of her time. In 1963, for instance, she had already spent his salary for 1968.

She won't mend his socks because he won't buy her a new mink coat. If he doesn't give a wrap, she doesn't give a darn.

He never realized how much she would want when he promised her before marriage that she would never want for anything.

She's a human gimme-pig.

What a woman! Without her, he'd never be what he is today—broke.

STRAYERS

She's more interested in spice than spouse.

She's a home-loving wife. When her husband is away, she's home loving another guy.

A couple of times he was crossed in love; then he married her, and was double-crossed.

His absence makes her heart go wander.

Her bathroom towels read, "His," "Hers," and "To Whom It May Concern."

She's getting indifferent—in different men's arms.

Every once in awhile, she feels like a new man.

While on vacation, she sent him a card reading: "Having wonderful time. Wish you were he."

He's interested in her happiness. In fact, he's so interested, he hired a detective to find out who was responsible for it.

He thought she was the salt of the earth until she started going with fellows with more pepper.

When he accused her of infidelity, she shouted indignantly, "That's an insult. I've been faithful to you dozens of times!"

He didn't mind her enjoying crackers in bed until he came home and discovered a crumb in the closet.

One night a week he goes out with the boys—on the other nights *she* goes out with them.

He's supposed to be brilliant, but he not only doesn't know everything, he doesn't even suspect anything.

When he travels, he doesn't understand that the XX's at the bottom of her letters means she's double-crossing.

She's leaving him for a crazy reason—she's crazy about another guy.

Woolgatherers

He wound up the cat, put out his wife, and got into bed with the clock.

He poured ketchup on his shoelaces and tied knots in his spaghetti.

He wears a wrist compass so he can tell whether he's coming or going.

He held an egg in his hand and boiled his watch three minutes.

He sent his wife to the bank, and kissed his money good-bye.

He picked up a snake and hit a stick.

He spent seven years studying why people are absent-minded. He finally came up with the answer—and promptly forgot it.

He rolled under the dresser and waited for his collar-button to find him.

He kissed his horse good-bye and hitched his wife to the plow.

He stood in front of a mirror for a half-hour trying to remember where he had seen himself before.

He took his wife out to dinner instead of his secretary.

Three months behind with his payments, he parked his car in front of the finance company's office.

He took a memory course and memorized one hundred phone numbers. Now he can't remember the names that go with them.

He slammed his wife and kissed the door.

He read an erroneous account of his death in the obituaries, and sent his wife a condolence card.

He dictated to his cigar and got his secretary lit.

He put the typewriter on his lap and started to unfasten the ribbon.

He fell overboard and forgot he could swim.

At her wedding, she told her corsage how lovely it looked, and threw her bridesmaid down the stairs.

Nicknames

They call her ALICE: her German parents took one look at her and said, *"Das ist Alles!"*

They call her AMAZON: she's so big at the mouth.

They call her APPENDIX: the fellows take her out once— that's enough.

They call him ARCH: he always needs support.

They call him ARCHITECT: when he meets a girl he's full of plans for her.

They call him ARCHEOLOGIST: his career lies in ruins.

They call him ARTIE: they hope he chokes.

They call her A.T. & T: she's always talking and talking.

They call him AUCTIONEER: he always looks forbidding.

They call him AVIATOR: he's a real high-flyer.

They call him BAKER: his career is one big loaf.

They call him BALDY: he's real smooth.

They call him BANANA: he's always getting skinned.

They call her BANJO: she's easy pickings.

They call him BARBER: he trims everyone he can.

They call her BASEBALL GIRL: she was thrown out at home.

They call her BEAN: anyone can string her.

They call him BLACKSMITH: he shoos his daughter's boy friends—out of the house.

They call her BOTTLER: when she goes for a fling no one can stopper.

They call him BOTTLETOP: he has a cork top and he's screwy.

They call him BOWLER: he builds himself up by knocking everyone down.

They call her BROWN SUGAR: she's so sweet and unrefined.

They call him BUTCHER: he's a real cut-up.

They call him BUTCHER: he's always giving everyone lots of tongue.

They call him BUTCHER: he's always scrimping to make both ends meat.

They call him BUTCHER: he's taking short cuts to wealth.

They call him BUS DRIVER: he tells everyone where to get off.

They call him CALVERT: he's so reserved.

They call her CARNIVAL QUEEN: she makes a lot of concessions.

They call him CARPENTER: he knows every vise in the book.

They call him CEMETERY: he's so grave.

They call her CHECKERS: she jumps when the boys make a wrong move.

They call him CHIROPODIST: he's always starting off on the wrong foot.

They call him CHIROPODIST: he's always down at the heels.

They call him CHIROPODIST: give him an inch and he takes the whole foot.

They call him CHOCOLATE BAR: he's half nuts.

They call her CINDERELLA: you have to slipper ten, slipper twenty.

They call him COLISEUM: he's a monumental ruin.

They call her COMMUNIST: all the fellows get their share.

They call him COMPOSITOR: he has such set ways.

They call him CONTRACEPTIVE: he's always evading the issue.

They call her CONTORTIONIST: she's always patting herself on the back.

They call him CORK: his head is always at the mouth of a bottle.

They call her CREAM OF WHEAT: she's so mushy.

They call him CUCUMBER: he's usually pickled.

They call him DENTIST: he bores everyone to tears.

They call him DENTIST: he lives from hand to mouth.

They call him DENTIST: he always looks down in the mouth.

They call him DENTIST: he works largely on nerve.

They call him DENTIST: he gets along on pull.

They call her DICTIONARY: she always has the last word.

They call her DINER: she likes to eat men's hearts out.

They call her DRAFTSMAN: she draws the lines on fellow's plans.

They call her DRESSMAKER: she's always making a slip.

They call her DRESSMAKER: she keeps the boys on pins and needles.

They call her DRESSMAKER: she knows the seamy side of life.

They call him DRUGGIST: he's a real pill.

They call him DRY CLEANER: he gets everyone all steamed up.

They call her DUSTY: she's been on the shelf so long.

They call her EASTER EGG: she's painted on the outside and hard-boiled inside.

They call her ECHO: she always has the last word.

They call her ELECTRICITY: she sure shocks 'em.

They call him ELEVATOR OPERATOR: he's always running people down.

They call her ESKIMO MAID: she always gives you the deep-freeze.

They call him FIREMAN: everyone tells him to go to blazes.

They call him FIREMAN: he never takes his eyes off the girls' hose.

They call him FLANNEL: he sure shrinks from washing.

They call her FLO: she talks in a steady stream.

They call her FLO: she has water on the knee and a creak in her back.

They call him FLORIST: he's going to seed.

They call her FLORIST: she's always showing her stems.

They call her FLORIST: she has Four Roses on her breath.

They call her FLOUR: she's been through the mill.

They call him FOOTBALL: everyone kicks him around.

They call him FOOTBALL: he's such a windbag.

They call her GARDENER: she knows all the rakes.

They call him HARPIST: he pulls strings to get ahead.

They call her HONEY: she has the hives.

They call him HOSPITAL ORDERLY: he's a real panhandler.

They call him JIGSAW: when faced with a problem he goes to pieces.

They call him JUNKMAN: he's always picking scraps.

They call him KING-KONG: he's always monkeying around.

They call her KITTY: she's dyed nine times.

They call him LAUNDRYMAN: he'll take the shirt off your back.

They call him LIBERTY BELL: he's half-cracked.

They call her LILY: she always goes out with dead ones.

They call him MAGICIAN: he walks down the street and turns into a saloon.

They call him MAGICIAN: he goes out fit as a fiddle and comes back tight as a drum.

They call her MAPLE SYRUP: she's such a sap.

They call him MASSEUR: he's always rubbing it in.

They call him MATZO: he's not well-bred.

They call him METEOROLOGIST: he can look at a girl and tell whether.

They call him MICROSCOPE: he magnifies everything.

They call her MINER: she makes the most of her natural resources.

They call her MOON: she's out all night.

They call him MOON: he becomes brighter the fuller he gets.

They call him MORTICIAN: life to him is a grave undertaking.

They call her MOTH: she's always chewing the rag.

They call him MUSICIAN: he's a playboy who's always making overtures.

They call him NERO: he's always fiddling around.

They call him NUDIST: you can never pin anything on him.

They call him NURSERYMAN: he's a professional grafter.

They call him OPTICIAN: two glasses and he makes a spectacle of himself.

They call him PARATROOPER: he falls down on the job.

They call him PAROLE: he interrupts you in the middle of a sentence.

They call him PAUL REVERE: he's always horsing around.

They call him PAWNBROKER: he makes advances.

They call him PHOTOGRAPHER: he sure can accentuate the negative.

They call him PILGRIM: he makes progress with women.

They call her POISON IVY: she's an awful thing to have on your hands.

They call her POSTMISTRESS: she's had lots of experience picking up males.

They call him PRESCRIPTION: he's always getting filled.

They call him PRETZEL MAKER: he makes crooked dough.

They call her PRINTER: she's real choosy, the way she picks her type.

They call him PSYCHIATRIST: he's always trying to get a girl on a couch.

They call him REALTOR: he has lots on his mind.

They call her ROBOT: she was made by a scientist.

They call him RUBBER BAND: he has an elastic conscience.

They call him QUITS: when he was born his parents decided to call it quits.

They call him SAILOR: he likes a little port in every girl.

They call her SANKA: there's no active ingredient in the bean.

They call him SANTA CLAUS: you should see the bags he runs around with.

They call him SANTA CLAUS: he won't leave women's stockings alone.

They call him SARDINE: he always lands in the can.

They call him SCULPTOR: he's some chiseler.

They call her SECONDHAND DEALER: she won't allow much on a sofa.

They call him SERUTAN: he's so backward.

They call her SEVEN-ELEVEN: she's so thin, when she walks you can hear her bones rattle.

They call him SHOEMAKER: he thinks he knows all.

They call him SHOWBOAT: he's been up the river so many times.

They call her SHOW GIRL: she's more show than girl.

They call her 6 DAY BIKE-RIDER: she finds it easy to make laps.

They call him SLIVER: he gets under everyone's skin.

They call him SNUFF MAKER: he puts his business in other people's noses.

They call him SPONGE: he's so flabby.

They call her STRETCH: she has an elastic conscience and a rubber neck.

They call him SUBWAY: he's a big bore.

They call him SURGEON: he's a real cut-up.

They call him SURRENDER: you take one look at him and give up.

They call him SYNCOPATION: his movements are irregular—from bar to bar.

They call him TAILOR: his policy is one of needles and threats.

They call him THEOPHILUS: he's theophilus-looking guy you ever met.

They call him TONSILITIS: he's a pain in the neck.

They call him TRAINMAN: he's plain loco and no motive.

They call him TROMBONIST: he's always blowing his own horn.

They call him UNDERTAKER: he has no use for anyone living.

They call her VILLAGE BELLE: everyone wants to wring her neck.

They call him WATCHMAN: both his eyes keep watching his nose.

They call him WEBSTER: words can't describe him.

They call him WHAT'S-IT: his father took one look at him when he was born, and yelled "What is it?"

They call her WILD-WEST GIRL: she comes into a room shooting from the lip.

They call her WINDOW DRESSER: she never pulls down the shade while dressing.

Squelches

I don't know what makes you tick, but I hope it's a time bomb.

I couldn't warm up to you if we were cremated together.

I don't know what I'd do without you, but I'd rather.

I can't think what I'll do without you, but it's worth a try.

The more I see of you, the worse I like you.

Don't you ever get tired of having yourself around?

Have a drink on me—a Mickey Finn.

Next time you pass my house, I'll appreciate it.

Why don't you get yourself X-rayed to see what people see in you?

You've got a fat chance to get me sore—and a head to match.

You're snappy on the comeback—like your checks.

Why don't you go on a diet, and quit eating my heart out?

Let's play horse. I'll be the front end—you just be yourself.

Why don't you take a long walk on a short pier?

I like you better the more I see you less.

The last time I met you was in a nightmare.

There's a biblical quotation, "Judas went out and hanged himself." And there's another: "Go thou and do likewise."

Why don't you blow your brains out? You've got nothing to lose.

Why don't you send your wits out to be sharpened?

Do me a favor—on your way home, please don't forget to jaywalk.

Let's play house. You be the door and I'll slam you.

Let's play Puss-in-the-corner. You stand in the corner and I'll kick you in the puss.

Please don't insist on telling me who you are. Let me detest you incognito.

If I've said anything to insult you, believe me, I've tried my best.

You have the manners of a gentleman. Tell me, to whom do they belong?

I can't remember your name, but your nasty manners are familiar.

I admit you're a distant relative. Trouble is you're not distant enough.

The sooner I never see you again, the better it'll be for both of us when we meet.

Let's go some place where we can each be alone.

I never forget a face, but in your case I'm willing to make an exception.

I'll swear eternal friendship for anyone who dislikes you as much as I do.

Don't go away—I want to forget you exactly as you are.

For a minute I didn't recognize you. It was the most enjoyable minute I ever spent.

I need a bookmark more than I need you. So step in front of a steamroller on your way out.

Stick around while I have a few drinks. It will make you so witty.

Stay with me—I want to be alone.

According to the theory of evolution, we're descended from either birds or monkeys. I don't see any feathers on you.

What's on your mind?—if you'll please excuse the exaggeration.

I'm sure you'll be all right—after the marijuana wears off.

Didn't I meet you in Las Vegas the day you blew your brains out?

Until you came along, I never saw a prune that exceeded six inches in diameter.

I understand you throw yourself into everything you undertake. Please go and dig a deep well.

I'm told you were down with a virus. I'm surprised it had a chance.

Your manners aren't half bad—they're all bad.

I'll be glad to have you over to my swimming pool—for a drowning lesson.

You know, you make me believe that man's descent from the ape hasn't started yet.

Look, there's a train pulling out shortly—get under it.

I hear you're taking lessons in deportment. Two more weeks and you'll be deported.

You look like the kind of person who throws himself into everything. I live over a lake—come and see me sometime.

You may be a social lion to your friends, but you're just an animal cracker to me.

You think you're such a great wit. Give me a couple of minutes to go out and check my brains—then we'll start even.

Don't tell me—I know who you are. You're the reason for birth control.

Just keep on talking, so I'll know what you're not thinking.

You're every other inch a gentleman.

Why don't you sue your brains for nonsupport?

Take some friendly advice—send your wits out to be sharpened.

You have a wonderful head on your shoulders—whose is it?

If they ever put a price on your head, take it.

Folks, he's a cousin of mine once removed. I only wish someone would remove him still further.

I'll bet your name is Webster. Words can't describe you.

I've got two minutes to kill, so tell me all you know.

I'm getting awfully cold—there's a breeze here stirred by a windbag.

Let's talk about your mind. On second thought, no matter.

You could make a good living hiring yourself out to haunt houses.

I recall your name all right, but I just can't force myself to think of your face.

You have a very striking face. How many times were you struck there?

You were given a nose to breathe through so that you could keep your mouth shut.

You're not really two-faced. If you had two, why would you be wearing that one?

If you want to save face, keep the lower half shut.

If I had your face, I'd pay a pickpocket to lift it.

What happened? Did an undertaker do an incomplete job on you?

Just remember—the mosquito that buzzes the loudest gets swatted first.

Years pass on, but you don't—more's the pity.

You have a nice head on your shoulders—too bad it's not on your neck.

Why don't you leave and let live?